The Financial Advisor M&A Guidebook

Greg Friedman · Shaun Kapusinski

The Financial Advisor M&A Guidebook

Best Practices, Tools, and Resources
for Technology Integration
and Beyond

palgrave
macmillan

Greg Friedman
Private Ocean
San Rafael, CA, USA

Shaun Kapusinski
HIFON LLC
Wadsworth, OH, USA

ISBN 978-3-030-00002-8   ISBN 978-3-030-00003-5   (eBook)
https://doi.org/10.1007/978-3-030-00003-5

Library of Congress Control Number: 2018958727

Cover image: © Andy Ryan/The Image Bank/Getty
Cover design by Tjaša Krivec

This Palgrave Macmillan imprint is published by the registered company Springer Nature Switzerland AG
The registered company address is: Gewerbestrasse 11, 6330 Cham, Switzerland

This book is dedicated to my Mother, Eleanor Duemling, and to my late Father,
C. Hugh Friedman, from where all of my success flows…
Greg Friedman

To Mariana, Jude, Eden, and Lila.
Shaun Kapusinski

Foreword

I have known Greg Friedman for many years. He is a man of many passions: his family, his friends and colleagues, music, the great outdoors, and business. Greg was raised by incredible parents who taught him how to live, love, and share; to be fully committed to whatever he chooses to do. He has led an incredibly fulfilled life in all respects. Now, why he would choose to go through the agony of writing a book for the financial industry makes me question whether he has learned anything along the way!

For those of us who share his passion for the business of financial advice, Greg's affliction is our gain. To create this book he partnered with Shaun Kapusinski, founder of HIFON (High Impact Financial Operations Network). Together Greg and Shaun have assembled a deeply-layered, practical approach to building, managing and operating a financial advisory business that will survive through transitions and last the next 100 years.

I know from whence I speak, having been in and around financial services for more than 40 years. I myself have suffered the pain of writing four books on a range of topics including mergers and acquisitions, strategy, structure, people, processes, and profits. I began as a reporter for a financial magazine, transitioned to investment management and research, built a successful practice management consulting business at Moss Adams LLP and now serve as a Managing Director at BNY Mellon Pershing, a significant part of the largest custodian in the world. Over my career, I have consulted with thousands of financial services firms throughout the USA, Europe, Canada, Australia, and, to a smaller degree, Asia and the Middle East.

I share my background to assure readers that I approached this book with a critical and cynical eye. I am pleased to report that I unequivocally recommend *The Financial Advisor M&A Guidebook*. Greg and Shaun's labor has delivered a well-formed and constructive explication of practice management, business leadership, and mergers and acquisitions in the new financial services industry.

Our industry has experienced a profound transformation over the last fifty years. In the 1960s, most RIAs were stock and bond pickers who executed trades through institutional brokers in return for research. Most retail-oriented financial professionals worked as employees of stock brokerage firms that paid them a commission for their work.

In the 1970s, the business began to shift from an investment-forward industry to a planning-forward profession, triggered in large part by the recognition of financial planning as a legitimate discipline. The Certified Financial Planner (CFP), Chartered Financial Consultant (ChFC) and Personal Financial Specialist (PFS) became accepted professional designations. CFP emerged from the investment world, ChFC from the insurance business and PFS from the accounting profession. Now we see a closer harmonization of these disciplines as financial professionals attempt to serve their clients holistically.

Also in the 1970s, Wall Street brokerage firms experienced a fundamental change in how they made money when the Justice Department and SEC ruled that fixed commissions were a form of collusion that disadvantaged investors. This ruling heralded the demise of many old-line firms, gave rise to the discount brokerage model and set the stage for a new type of broker/dealer—the independent contractor. This model shifted brokers from a controlled process of selling proprietary products to a supervised independent structure wherein registered reps have access to an investment marketplace not solely manufactured by their own firms.

These developments planted the seeds that gave rise to the retail RIA movement. Financial professionals soon realized that under the Securities Act of 1940, they could operate under a fiduciary standard rather than a simpler suitability standard. They could become professional buyers instead of professional sellers. They could establish their own independent businesses and purchase services from other providers including custodians, financial technology companies, and outsourced investment management firms.

Today, RIA firms account for almost 30% of total retail assets (Cerulli Associates, 2018). The average size of RIA firms continues to rise and the rate of consolidation continues to grow. Each year, the industry witnesses hundreds of mergers and acquisitions, many funded by private equity investment and others created by strategic combinations of like-minded firms.

As a result, retail wealth management continues to evolve. Practices are becoming businesses. Advisors are becoming managers. Single-location firms are becoming part of branch networks. And managing the balance sheet is becoming as important as the income statement.

In other words, we are entering a new period of complexity that may challenge the entrepreneurs among us. Many probably envisioned fewer headaches and fewer people to be accountable to when making the move to "independence." Independence has morphed into interdependence, however, with the critical necessity of choosing and collaborating with strategic partners. Integrating this technology during a merger or acquisition requires thorough planning and precise execution, all with the underlying goal of enhancing the client and employee experience.

The Financial Advisor M&A Guidebook will become one of your most valuable resources as you enter a merger or acquisition. Herein Greg and Shaun outline a linear process for this complicated transition, offering insight and advice for every step, anticipating dangerous areas and pointing the way to a smooth integration.

I find it refreshing that individuals who have gained so much from their careers in financial services are so eager to help others create successful businesses. Truthfully, I would not have expected anything less from Greg and Shaun.

It is a privilege to be asked to write the Foreword for *The Financial Advisor M&A Guidebook*. The journey to an enduring financial advisory firm requires careful navigation. Thankfully, firms may now draw on this valuable reference as they work to overcome obstacles, achieve milestones, and construct a better workplace and client experience.

Jersey City, NJ, USA
Mark C. Tibergien
Chief Executive Officer and Managing Director,
Pershing Advisor Solutions, LLC, BNY Mellon

Preface

I have been fortunate to lead somewhat of a double life professionally. It has been the best of both worlds, having access to information and an incredible variety of people which has afforded a unique experience in this industry. Working in financial services for over 30 years, much of that time starting and building my own wealth management firm while along the way owning and building a fintech firm, I've seen monumental change in all aspects of what we do to help our clients live happier, more fulfilling lives.

Technology's role in our industry since the early days has gone from an afterthought, to something "interesting," to a critical and necessary priority for our business. It defines how we do what we do and if used properly, it can elevate a firm as it grows, working alongside us almost as a real, flesh and blood member of the team. But that's harder to achieve than it sounds. Technology can also be an unwieldy adversary that causes more frustration than efficiency and a significant business cost if not given the appropriate amount of attention and time investment. Throw into that a second level of technology during a merger or acquisition and you're sitting on a ticking time bomb that could threaten to bring your newly established firm's operations to a grinding halt.

I'm not trying to use scare tactics here, but speaking from experience, the distractions and costs associated with poor technology strategy and decisions can be enormous! When Friedman & Associates merged with Salient Financial in 2009 to become Private Ocean, we felt confident that we had checked all the right boxes. We had done our homework. Before we ever signed anything, we had extensive, ongoing in-person meetings, discussing everything from our values and philosophy on financial advice to analyzing our processes, our operations, our technology, and our people. We considered it a marriage—one that would go the distance and evolve with intention. As an outspoken advocate for technology, we even took a closer look at how both firms used their systems and how they would need to adapt over time.

But there was no guide, no checklist, no warnings or red flags, and no "right" way to pull off the technology integration that turned into an enormous part of our merger. Despite our best efforts to find materials on this, there simply wasn't anything available at the time. Frankly, we assumed that given the lack of information available, this process must not be that difficult—and did we underestimate the challenges!

Which brings me to the purpose of this book. To say technology is at the heart of what we do is an understatement. A huge one. On the surface, it seems secondary to our relationships and our focus on clients and people and what really matters. But it *is* the central vehicle that we all use to accomplish our goals, stay competitive, and scale upward. Our goal with this book is to help firms avoid costly mistakes that can have lasting, damaging effects on a firm's future.

When I started talking to Shaun Kapusinski, an operations specialist and fellow fintech-aficionado, we had already met a few times at industry conferences over the years, exchanging stories and lessons learned about integrating technology within merged firms. On one occasion at an advanced leadership conference, we sat outside and had drinks and talked shop, realizing quickly that we had a mutual passion in moving our industry forward through shared information and experiences. Those conversations turned into ideas that we thought would be helpful for other firms in our position. I felt confident that he was the perfect partner to help write this book, as he is both of the "new-guard," and brings the right combination of forward-thinking process with hands-on experience helping firms navigate all of the aspects of integration. I know I would have benefitted having him as an advisor in some of my M&A dealings.

As for what you can expect in the chapters ahead, we've broken down the book to mirror the cycle of how you would naturally approach technology integration before and after a merger or acquisition. We will walk you through the steps of strategy, timing, assessment, implementation, adoption, and growth, all while considering how to best inspire and galvanize a firm's most valuable asset—its people. I will share my own personal experiences and tips as I have applied them in my firm's M&A activities, and Shaun will provide a more operational, hands-on perspective to help you proactively plan, assess and execute.

This guide is obviously suitable for firms in the midst of an M&A event. However, we've intentionally designed this guide to offer *all* advisors a glimpse into what lies ahead for them, something tangible to digest before you enter into a merger or acquisition. Maybe you've only started to crack the surface of what M&A looks like for you. Maybe it's not even on your radar now. This book may help you understand what's involved and help shape your approach.

And while we do want this book to serve as a technology integration guide for firms preparing for, considering or in the middle of M&A activity, we will certainly touch upon other key components as so many factors tend to overlap. Along the way, we'll include opinions and insights from some of our partners, intermediaries, and colleagues.

We hope you find this guide useful, practical, and easy to apply to your situation. We are honored to be able to share our stories from the trenches of a number of M&A transitions and offer you honest, candid insight into what really happens before and after you sign on the dotted line from a technology perspective.

San Rafael, USA   Greg Friedman

Acknowledgements

This book is the product of an enormous team effort, inspired by the enlightening and sometimes challenging personal experiences of a number of M&A transactions over the years. While we recognize that every deal is unique, our hope was that in sharing a variety of our own uncensored stories—the good, the bad, and the ugly—we could help guide other advisors down a wiser path to achieving their goals.

First off, I'd like to thank Mark Tibergien for continuing to offer his wisdom and leadership for our industry. He is the model to which we all strive—an innovator, a collaborator, a colleague, and, personally, a friend. His spirit for elevating our profession is part of the fabric of our collective success—and he does this with class and humor!

I would also like to thank Shaun Kapusinski for his tireless work on creating this guide, outlining in detail his steps for helping firms find their footing as they wade into uncharted M&A waters. His passion for serving others and his dedication to helping advisors succeed certainly gives me great confidence in the future of our industry.

I would not be sharing these experiences today if it were not for the many amazing people who I have been privileged to work with—from those at Junxure, Friedman & Associates, Salient Wealth Management, Lakeview Financial, and of course, Private Ocean. In particular, I'd like to thank Angela Giombetti and Cynthia Greenfield for their hard work and help with this book. I am always in awe of everyone's tremendous willingness to take on challenges in a positive way and their creativity in getting things done for the sake of taking great care of clients.

There are other leaders in this industry who should be acknowledged for their continued stewardship for advisors, whether to educate on M&A trends or to help shepherd us toward the latest technology. To David DeVoe, Dan Seivert, Joel Bruckenstein, Michael Kitces, Bob Veres and so many others, we thank you for your commitment to helping all of us improve.

Last but certainly not least, I am so grateful for my family—my wife, Laurie, and my twins, Andrew and Marissa—who keep me grounded and teach me every day.

Greg Friedman

There are many people who have been on the proverbial sidelines, cheering me on, leading up to and throughout the process of writing of this book. To each of you, I would like to share my gratitude.

To Tom Haught, Gerry Knotek, and Trevor Chuna for the opportunities I've had, under your guidance, with the Sequoia team to help grow our firm. I'm grateful for the experience and confidence our many acquisitions have given me, which allowed me to be in a position to write this book.

To Greg Friedman, who had a vision for this book and a drive to pursue it. Though initially encouraging me to write on my own, I'm grateful he decided we should do this together. It's a privilege to write alongside him.

To Ann Massey, John Convery, Angela Wright, Maria Hinton, and Rob Siegmann, who were willing to start a small study group with me back in 2010, it's because of this group that HIFON has become what it is today. Thank you for starting this journey with me.

To my entire network through HIFON. I am grateful you are here. A special recognition to those members who provided stories, experiences, and lessons to share throughout this book.

To Lisa Crafford, who started her small study group back in 2012 and then told Bob Veres all about it. And to Bob and his wife, Jean Sinclair, for inviting Lisa and me to his practice management conference to speak about our groups; and then later, for involving me in the operations track of Insider's Forum. It was at this conference where Greg and I met. I couldn't be more grateful for that introduction.

To Ian Crafford, Andrew Bodjanac, Aden Pavkov, and Michael Humphrey, thank you for your advice to pursue this book and your encouragement when I didn't think it was something I could do.

Thank you to the many friends and family members who played a role as both HIFON, and later this book, became a reality: Adam Rissmiller, Geoff

Moore, Levi Welling, Alan Moore, Michael Kitces, Steve Stelkic, and Chris Spillmann.

To the awesome writing team of Angela Giombetti, Cynthia Greenfield, and Sonya Spillmann. For Angela's superb skill at weaving two authors together; Cynthia's experience with Greg and Private Ocean; and for Sonya, my sister, who took my thoughts, made sense of them, and wrote them out on the page.

To Jude, Eden, and Lila, you are my world. To Mariana, without you, all of this would be nothing. Most importantly, I am grateful for the love and grace of Jesus Christ, my Lord and Savior. None of this would have been possible on my own.

Shaun Kapusinski

Disclosures

The views and opinions expressed in this book by the authors are their own and do not necessarily reflect the view of any former, current, or future employers.

Contents

About the Authors

Greg Friedman is an innovator and advocate for excellent wealth management. He is co-founder and CEO of Private Ocean, one of the West Coast's leading wealth management firms. He's also the former co-founder of Junxure, an industry-leading CRM for advisors. Friedman is widely recognized as one of the nation's top financial advisors. *Investment Advisor Magazine* named him as one of its Top 25 most influential financial advisors in 2008, 2009, and 2010. In 2008, *Financial Planning Magazine* included Friedman in its elite list of financial "Movers and Shakers." In 2007, Charles Schwab honored him with its prestigious IMPACT Award® for "Best in Tech." Friedman plays a lead role in the movement toward tighter technology integration in the financial planning industry. He was also recognized by Investment News in 2017 as an Icon and Innovator.

Shaun Kapusinski is all about operational excellence. He has spent over 15 years at Sequoia Financial Group, LLC, and is currently a Director of Operations focusing on technology and administration. Kapusinski turned his passion for operations into one of the industry's first operations-focused study groups. In 2010, he founded HIFON, an RIA operations network linking together over 200 RIA firms across the country. Shaun's other industry and community involvement includes being a member of The University of Akron's Finance Advisory Board; he is a current Committee Member for the operations track at Bob Veres' Insider's Forum; and he is a former member of the Schwab Advisor Services Technology, Operations and Service Advisory Board. Shaun has been a speaker on various operations topics at multiple industry conferences. www.hifon.org.

List of Tables

1

The M&A Landscape and Technology's Role

Like any maturing industry, the financial services industry realized somewhere along the way that joining forces was a powerful means to grow and grow quickly. I'm simplifying tremendously, of course, as a number of factors created this perfect storm that has paved the way for the sharp increase in M&As among financial advisory firms. I'll get to that in a minute, but it is a safe assumption to say that today M&A is a key consideration for advisors whether it's part of a development strategy, succession plan, or retirement plan.

Broken Records: The Current M&A Landscape

Rather than look too far behind us, let's examine the numbers today. According to M&A consultants, ECHELON Partners, a record number of M&A deals—168—closed in the advisor space in 2017, representing a 22% growth over the previous record set in 2016. Aside from a fifth straight year of record highs in M&A activity, the size of the deals has also increased, with average acquisitions involving wealth managers exceeding $1.01 billion in assets under management.[1] In 2018, Both ECHELON Partners and another

---

[1] ECHELON Partners (2017) *2017 RIA M&A Deal Report*. Echelon-Partners.com. Accessed 8 July 2018.

© The Author(s) 2018
G. Friedman and S. Kapusinski, *The Financial Advisor M&A Guidebook*,
https://doi.org/10.1007/978-3-030-00003-5_1

leading M&A consulting firm, DeVoe & Co., reported a record-setting boost in the first quarter (DeVoe recorded 47 deals[2] and ECHELON, 46), and both firms believe that trend will continue.

These numbers may not seem terribly significant if you consider there are *12,172* SEC-registered advisors as of April 1, 2017,[3] according to a report from Investment Adviser Association and National Regulatory Services (NRS). But these figures don't consider deals that go unreported or the firms either starting to consider M&A as part of their growth strategy or the ones already in negotiations. Speaking from experience, the last firm we acquired had been through several previous transactions that were not recorded and we know this isn't unusual. Rather than note just the firms who have reported deals, the question to ask is, how many of those *12,172* firms are considering M&A activity over the next 5–10 years?

With M&A becoming such a hot topic and only getting hotter, it's important to understand how and why we got here. There are a handful of contributing factors, and while these are certainly not inclusive, here are a few based on our personal experiences, interviews with our peers and from research firms like DeVoe & Co. and ECHELON Partners.

- **Competition**. It is an extremely competitive market out there today, and that should not come as a surprise. The financial services industry is maturing and has been highly profitable for many, many years, with the demand from wealth clients far outstripping the number of advisors available to serve them. In addition, today's client is more tech-savvy, informed, and interested in being involved in their finances. They're also shopping around online at multiple firms. While that means the more recognized value of wealth managers, it also means the rise of robo-advisors and DIYers, making it difficult to compete when so many online tools are available for free or next to nothing.
- **A Tough Regulatory Environment**. The ever-changing regulatory climate is one that takes serious resources and skills to navigate successfully. The challenges we face today with compliance and regulations are time-consuming and stressful, and the liability for giving advice is not unlike an obstacle course.
- **High Valuations**. This ongoing bull market (as of Q3 2018) has created a very attractive environment for advisors. RIA valuations are high as are

---

[2]DeVoe & Co. (2018) *DeVoe RIA Deal Book, Q1 2018*. DevoeandCompany.com. Accessed 8 July 2018.

[3]Investment Adviser Association and National Regulatory Services (2017) *2017 Evolution Revolution*. https://www.investmentadviser.org/publications/evolution-revolution. Accessed 8 July 2018.

the number of interested buyers who see short and long-term benefits of scale and depth. Combine that with many wealth managers eyeing retirement and succession, and everyone sees a winning solution.

- **The Allure of More Independence**. An important component of M&A activity involves the breakaway firm. Breakaway activity has continued to gain momentum through 2018 as pressure mounts to move due to increased Broker Protocol defections. According to ECHELON Partner's RIA M&A Deal Report, there has been a 6% increase in breakaways in the first quarter of 2018 compared to the fourth quarter of 2017.
- **The Allure of Less Independence**. Perhaps an outcome of some of the other factors, some advisors are finding the evolving RIA landscape overwhelming and difficult to sustain, especially if there is no succession or retirement plan in place. Riding out market volatility can get tiresome, technology can be daunting to stay current, and recruiting and retaining advisors can be challenging. There is power in numbers and partnering with others or handing over control provides those advisors with peace of mind that their firm and their clients will be in good hands. It also offers the financial security to step away when the time comes.

Whatever a firm's reason for considering and entering into the M&A waters, the question often comes down to growth. Organic growth has gotten harder in recent years, and advisors have had to get creative to stay competitive. Joining forces, acquiring or selling are all viable options to achieve those growth goals in one transaction. But it's not like going on a blind date. The amount of screening, planning, and interviewing involved is extensive on the front end and should continue during and after the M&A process. A firm also needs to consider how to prepare, position, and present its best self—from its people, its organization, its processes and of course, and its technology resources.

Technology: A Key Component of M&A

For many advisors in smaller or even mid-sized firms, it only takes a handful of missteps during a merger or acquisition to jeopardize their business. A significant and often overlooked component to a successful RIA merger or acquisition is the thoughtful integration of technology.

Technology is often a word that advisors use with purpose but without a deeper understanding of the impact it truly has on our business. It's a nebulous concept, morphing, and shifting with every day, making it harder and harder to know when to leap on to something new. Is it hardware? Software?

Apps? You may do your research and feel good about committing to a system today, but what happens tomorrow when the next "ground-breaking" fintech is unveiled? Unfortunately, this never-ending cycle of shiny new things can become paralyzing, and the next thing you know, you're using horse and buggy technology that makes it twice as difficult to catch up. Pairing that with a second firm's technology in a merger and acquisition can be disruptive and downright painful. Like it or not, if you're not leveraging technology and exploring new ways to attract business organically you are going to get left behind in more ways than one.

There are all sorts of guides on the market on how to approach M&A—the art of the deal, the meeting of the minds, comparing philosophy, and having the right conversations, looking at balance sheets and numbers and growth and all that. But there is no guide for how to navigate technology integration between two firms. Why is that? Our industry is a unique animal, but the reasons we might overlook technology are fairly common.

- **We Take It for Granted**. We live in a world now where things are just supposed to work. Remember the "Easy Button?" You turn on your computer, you log in, and an enormous amount of complex data is at your fingertips. That feeling of security extends to our personal lives, too. You can check your home's security and temperature with an app. You have weather, music, and an encyclopedia of random knowledge on-demand courtesy of our virtual assistants, Alexa and Siri. This isn't generation-based, either. My 83-year-old mother is on Facebook sharing videos with the ease of a millennial.
- **We Are in the Business of People First**. Our industry prides itself on being people-focused. We like to think we are the opposite of automated. Except we're not. Technology helps us accomplish many of the things that our clients find valuable. Real-time financial advice based on the absolute latest numbers. Information on-demand. Reports that are easy to generate and understand. And historical data on our clients and their families that help us get to know them and serve them better.
- **Technology Growth Is Organic**. And lastly, technology is a tricky, ever-evolving animal. It's not one and done, like signing a lease on a bigger office space and turning on the lights. You're never done growing along with your technology, and no two firms grow the same. It touches every aspect of our business, evolves gradually and usually out of necessity. I assure you that the technology you started with on day one of your business looks a lot different than your tools today.

Before, during and after an M&A event, technology plays a key role in valuation, in organization, and in establishing and presenting how you run your business. It's not unlike a buyer looking into real estate. A buyer would be more attracted to a home that's been kept up to date and find it even more valuable if that home has things like solar panels, high-tech security, a sophisticated sprinkler system, and other smart technology. In other words, knowing that a seller has been thoughtful in its upgrades that are designed to serve the home today and in the future is very reassuring.

Applied to our business, a firm that has a well-organized CRM that can provide data instantly and accurately offers a similar reassurance. A modern, user-friendly client portal that is easily customizable for the future shows intention, efficiency, and dedication to evolving client needs. Perhaps most importantly in the M&A sense, high-use, streamlined, and thoughtful use of technology translates to a culture of agility and innovative thinking—two appealing characteristics for a firm looking to buy, sell or merge.

The chart below compares technology usage in an advisory firm at its most basic form versus a firm that maximizes its applications across all aspects from customer relationship management systems (CRM) to a client portal. The result may impact not only a firm's efficiency and service levels but also its valuation during an M&A assessment (Table 1.1).

Now, to be clear, technology isn't a deal-breaking factor for M&A, but it's definitely one that advisors underestimate. Often, we are enamored with the art of the deal and overlook some of the operational inefficiencies that exist in both the other firm and our own. The goal is to properly assess what you'll be dealing with on the other side of the fence and prepare accordingly.

Technology integration discussions should ideally kick off during the negotiation phase of M&A—far before you close the deal—but chances are, no matter when you decided to address the integration, your personal approach to technology had some impact on how you selected the other firm for this transaction. Intentionally or not, you considered the other firm's tools and processes, and gauged their people's efficiency and agility to accept change.

As we jump into the first stage of navigating technology integration—strategy—it's important to start with the end goal in mind. What are you trying to achieve and how will organizing and investing time in your technology get you there? What metrics matter most to you? What does success look like to you after this integration, the next one, and in two, five, even ten years? Creating your wish list is a great place to start before diving in to create your strategic roadmap.

Table 1.1 Technology comparison

Installed technology	Incrementally positive attributes	Baseline technology
Customer Relationship Management System	Web-based CRM with extensive data, activities, and notes for all clients	A data source containing client contact information
Performance Reporting System	Performance reporting system with significant historical data connected to custodians receiving daily reconciled transactional data	No substitute
Trading & Rebalancing System	Integrated model-based trading & rebalancing system allowing models, models of models, integrated ebalancing alerts, and ax harvesting	Simple model creation and management with the ability to export trades to custodial trading systems
Financial Planning System	Holistic, multi goal, Monte Carlo-based financial planning integrated with custodial and held away assets	Single goal-based financial planning
Client Portal	Secure, web-based client portal reporting both the advisor-managed and held away assets, balances, transactions, and performance	No substitute
Data Integration	Extensive data integration of custodial systems, held away assets, and all of the system above to reduce data entry, errors, and differing data	Basic custodial data integration

2

Aligning Your Technology Strategy

Here you are. Perhaps you've already taken the leap and you're in that first exciting stage of your merger or acquisition. Maybe you're just starting talks with a firm that seems like a good fit for you and your growth strategy. Or maybe you're a team player, a consultant who specializes in practice management or a parent company looking for resources to help firms navigate the M&A waters with minimal disruption. No matter the flavor of the deal or your role, the outcome is the same. You need to get on the same page and become one firm—not just in name, but in philosophy, process, attitude, culture, and of course, technology systems.

First off, let's just acknowledge the inherent challenges we all have with technology, from vetting and choosing the best tools, to implementation, to adoption, and getting good ROI over time. It seems like a never-ending project to stay current, compliant, and efficient, and at times, technology can be both a blessing and curse for operations. Merging two firms with two different tech stacks seems like twice the battle, but it doesn't have to be.

Getting started on the right track to technology integration means creating a dedicated strategy and roadmap—one with key milestones and benchmarks—that sets expectations and outlines roles and responsibilities. Before that, however, you'll need to know your destination. Ask yourself these high-level questions:

© The Author(s) 2018
G. Friedman and S. Kapusinski, *The Financial Advisor M&A Guidebook*,
https://doi.org/10.1007/978-3-030-00003-5_2

- What are you trying to do with your new firm? Growth? Succession?
- Who is your client base (and even more importantly who are the clients you will be going for in the future) and how will you protect their experience? How will you attract and delight your clients of the future?
- What are you trying to accomplish with your technology?

If you didn't emphasize technology integration before you closed the deal, the strategy stage is a great place to start to address expectations. Assessing will play a large role on the front end, and then you'll dive into discovery. Who uses what tools and how? How do people's roles align with the technology you use?

I think it's critical during this stage to listen to the people in the trenches and find out what works well and not so well. You'll also assess attitudes, aptitudes, and capacity. How capable and available are your team? How flexible are they in roles that may evolve quickly or over time? When we're talking about people in any role—we ask them how something is working today. But let me ask you a different question. Is it scalable? Would your operations work in a $5B firm the same as it does in a $1.6B firm? When we're assessing people and technology during an integration, look at the bones of your architecture.

We often say, "What got you here won't get you there," and in action, you'll need to remind yourself that to get to the next phase of your firm's future, you'll need to be nimble and ready to build the right support structure.

In this chapter, I'll share my approach to communication and discuss cultural considerations after which Shaun will cover his operational approach to developing a technology strategy. We'll also offer our shared "wild cards"—factors you might not see coming during this stage but should always anticipate.

Communication: Your Most Powerful Tool

There is no such thing as over-communication between two merging firms during the strategy phase of tech integration. Many acquisitions happen quickly while some have the luxury of more adequate amounts of time. Either way, communicate early and often about what's going on. In order for both teams to accept and adjust before any new implementation, offer as much information as you can with as much lead time as possible about anticipated changes.

Bringing two firms together is a little like bringing two families together. Each family operates differently and every member has their own personality and responsibilities. The more you share, the faster you and your team can assess your current situation and create a clear, productive plan to move forward together.

At this early stage, don't be afraid to dive a little deep in conversations on the philosophical end of technology integration. Meaning, how does the other firm's investment strategy and philosophy affect how they approach and implement technology? Both firms might say, for example, that delivering excellent client service is their biggest priority. But you need to go deeper to understand how people operate and what motivates them. The goal here is to gain a clearer picture of your newly expanded team, their approach to their work, the tools that they use, and their expectations. From there, you can begin shaping your tech strategy.

Breaking the Ice

The people involved in these conversations will likely go beyond your leadership team and extend into your operations, IT, and client service staff. In some circumstances, these are people who were not part of the M&A negotiations and they may be meeting their counterparts for the first time. Here are a few exercises to break the ice and find common ground.

At Private Ocean, we set up initial one-hour meetings with various blended teams to provide overall guidance on our expectations and where we're headed. We also use this time to simply have a conversation and get to know each other. These are casual, personal gatherings with a loose agenda but focused on getting to know each other. We ask general questions of everyone and talk big picture of the firm we intend to be. Everyone has a voice, and all ideas are welcome.

Now, it's human nature to be impatient in the beginning of this process as you've just closed this firm-changing deal and want to get it moving as soon as possible. There's also an expected sense of limbo for at least half of your new staff. Often, we have seen advisors make assumptions, skip the communication and consideration phase and go right to execution out of impatience. Resist the urge to make hasty decisions! Investing the time up front to lay out a strategy will set you and your team up for a smoother road ahead.

Initial Cultural Considerations

I've often referred to the common adage that culture trumps strategy every time. Part of the strategy is to get a solid feel for the firm's culture. Considering that culture is defined as the norms of behavior, actions, communication and thinking patterns which define what is and is not acceptable, a business' culture cannot be ignored in lieu of its strategic plans—no matter how dynamic the leader or robust its systems.

Culture isn't something you can spot right away, but with every meeting, every conversation, and every interaction you can begin to observe how people's actions align to their values. Here are a few factors to keep in mind when assessing culture and its impact on technology (Table 2.1).

The answers you receive during the strategy phase are neither good nor bad—they are data points. And the more data you have at this early stage, the better prepared you will be for the transition.

Now that you've begun developing a rapport through open communication and considered cultural considerations across both firms, it's time to hand things over to operations. In this next section, Shaun offers his deep dive approach to strategy on people, processes, and technology.

Table 2.1 Culture's impact on technology

Attitude	Aptitude	Consistency
How is technology discussed in meetings and between employees? Is it a nuisance? Is it treated like oxygen? Based on your observation, how would you describe the other firm's outlook on technology as it relates to their business? Do people speak their opinions?	How well and how deeply do your new colleagues use their technology? Are they excited to embrace change for the growth of the firm, or do they shy away from new ideas and processes? Is technology viewed as a growth propellant or a barrier?	Is the use of technology consistent across the entire hierarchy? Is everyone using the systems the same way or are there exceptions? Is there a sense of governance over usage so that if and when things change, everyone will be able to adapt and still get what they need?

How Size Matters: Big Fish vs. Little Fish

How much does the size of a firm impact its M&A outcomes and its road to technology integration? The short answer—immensely. As the ECHELON Partners report noted, the average M&A event in 2017 was a big one—$1.01B. Whether you're a larger firm acquiring a smaller one, a single practitioner selling internally to an existing employee, a breakaway, or a medium-sized firm merging with a similar one, size can definitely impact your road to integration.

I compare it to raising children. Both Shaun and I are parents, and as a father to twins, I can tell you from experience that the challenges multiply greatly with each child. If raising one child has its unique set of challenges, raising two is three times as much, and so on. In the M&A perspective, if a sole advisor is acquiring another single-person firm or buying their book of business, the process to integrate is much less complex and easier to address than the acquisition of a larger firm of 20 people. The advantage to managing a small group is that you have a much tighter information loop; there is an exponential amount of change and complexity when you add size.

The size and influence of the acquiring firm matters most during the strategy stage. While tech "integration" is often discussed, it's relevant to ask if both firms will be evaluated for their technology best practices. Will you try to integrate the best of both worlds or will the acquiring firm's processes and technology stay the standard? In our experience, there is a huge benefit in asking, "Who is doing good work here and can we use this?" In fact, our approach has been to consistently look from a strategic sense at where we are building toward and what technology tools will help us be successful. This may mean that the right solution is one that is new to the entire organization. We'll discuss this more in later chapters.

The Role of Operations

At HIFON (High Impact Financial Operations Network), we often say that the operations strategy is about discovery. During the strategy stage, you are forming an initial matrix for how best to manage the integration process. This stage is akin to finding the corner and edge pieces of a puzzle; the more questions you ask and answers you receive, the better framework you'll have before getting to work on the rest of the puzzle pieces that you'll need to fit in later.

I've heard it over and over in my experience helping firms through M&A integrations: early involvement of operations can greatly influence the planning and implementation phase, which will benefit both the owners and staff. How so?

Asking questions gives you a clear idea of who and what you are working with. You can discern how each firm feels about where they are and where they want to be moving forward. Finding out as much information as you can early on sets you up to proactively affect the combined firm's direction for a successful integration.

Checklists are invaluable to anyone in operations, but there isn't a one-size-fits-all checklist in the strategy phase. Here, robust checklists aren't your most valuable tool—you are.

People, Processes, and Technology

At this stage, you need to know: How are the people, processes, and technology utilized, valued, and developed at this firm? You can anticipate how the firm will respond if those in leadership aren't regularly adhering to firm-wide expectations of technology adoption and application. You are assessing if it's an environment where adoption is going to be a challenge or if the firm regularly makes changes with an easily adaptable staff. Is there adherence to the firm's strategic plans?

People

 The first thing to assess is what the team members mean to the firm and how they are utilized. Ask questions about how the people fit in—from the perspective of both the owners and the clients. Keep your endpoint in mind: your goal is to devise a plan to deliver the firm's services while best utilizing the talents and resources of a future unified team.

- **Who Is In Charge**: Who are the decision makers when it comes to people, processes, and technology? Who drives strategy? Who drives change? Are the change agents of the firm the owners, managers, or others?
- **Mindset of Growth or Maintenance**: What investments are made into the people? Firms in a growth mindset often undergo change more often and readily than firms in a maintenance mode. Typically, growth firms will invest in their people for their personal and professional development in order to maximize firm productivity. On the other hand, nongrowth firms may fall into ruts of procedure, maintaining a culture of not investing in their people or valuing technology enhancements.
- **Attitudes and Opinions**: Across the board, change can be challenging—for individuals as well as groups. Find out how their team has dealt with change before and generally how the owners think people will feel about moving forward.

Who's in Charge Here?

During all aspects of the M&A process, it's important for everyone to know who is leading the charge and ultimately making the big decisions. The structure of your deal will determine if both firms have a say or if the acquiring firm ultimately makes the final choices. As I look back on our first acquisition, some of our integration efforts seemed arduous because there was a lack of clarity and to who was ultimately making the decisions. We were tripping over each other to get along with our new colleagues and trying not to be the "alpha dog." What would have been more effective as the acquiring firm is if on Day 1 we were more assertive. It doesn't mean you need to throw your weight around, it just means everyone is clear about the structure steering the wheel. Every ship needs a captain (or captains) and those people need to be determined ahead of time.

Process

Next, gauge the current processes in place. Not only do you want to know who does what, but how everything from new business to ongoing client maintenance is accomplished. Here you will ask general process questions related to customer service, financial planning, investment philosophies, and trade execution. You want to know what processes are in place for every team, department, and role.

- **What Strategies Are Employed Currently**: You're trying to get a feel for how things are done. Is the strategy that advisors are the only ones in contact with clients? Does technology provide efficiencies for everyone's role? Is retention through personal development and individual empowerment a part of the growth plan?
- **How People Interact**: Do the advisors rely heavily on the support staff or are they autonomous? Are teams, groups, or pods developed and is that part of the current strategic plan? Have departments or committees been established to allow for subject matter expertise?
- **Compliance and Uniformity**: Do many advisors request individualized reports or ask for unique requests? Do a few advisors independently do the work other advisors delegate to their operations team? How often are exceptions made to the standards? And when, if ever, is it allowed?

Technology

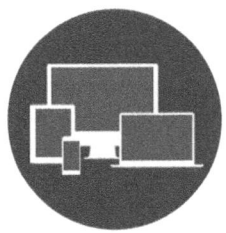

Third, you want to get a feel for how the firm currently uses technology. Ideally, technology is used consistently from top to bottom with the same roadmap and strategy. If the firm's top people regularly utilize existing technology according to firm standards, it will be a clear indicator of the rest of the firm's willingness and attitude toward adapting to potentially new tech standards.

But if the firm's leaders don't use their technology as intended, you want to know why. In addition, start thinking and anticipating what this may mean moving forward. For example, if the president wants technology built outside of what is standard, it's safe to anticipate other staff will want (and expect) exceptions to be made. So, ask about how tech use (or non-use) lines up with stated technology objectives.

You want to get a feel if technology is an optional method to keep track of a minimal amount of data or if it's a powerful and indispensable tool utilized by every member of the firm, top to bottom.

- **Technology Drivers**: Is there a technology officer, lead person, or committee in place who makes decisions about standards and usage? Is there a technology roadmap? If so, how many years are mapped out by the firm? (1, 3, or 5 years?) Depending on the answer, you'll know if the firm has a long-term or short-term vision already in place.
- **Flexibility vs. Rigidity**: What is the feeling toward the amount of flexibility in their systems, or in contrast, the rigidity of current tech standards? When there are few exceptions, you can ascertain that the firm values standard procedures. In certain cases, though, this can also mean there is little willingness to be flexible, which is often needed in a growing firm with many types of advisors and clients. In contrast, if there are numerous exceptions to standards, it could be a flag that there's an absence of a unified strategy for technology usage.
- **Client Experience**: What role does technology play for their clients? Does the firm want their clients to have a navigable website and the ability to speak directly with staff? Do they want client information to be easily accessible on mobile devices? How much control does the firm want to keep versus how autonomous and empowered do they want their clients to feel?

After asking these questions, inquire again about tech usage expectations. It's not unusual for additional issues to come up on a second pass. After a bit more probing, there may be clear differences in consistency than what was initially communicated. You want to possess the most accurate information about the firm before moving into the planning phase.

Friedman's 5: The Tech Integration Players

 In any M&A event, you're likely to encounter certain personalities that can impact the integration process. There is no right or wrong way to structure your approach, only the opportunity to better understand how two firms can work together to achieve a shared goal.

1. **The Committee**. Often with mid-size to larger firms, decisions are made by committee. This would include the 100% owners, the founders, the C-suite executives, and principals. People often error on the side on not including enough people in pre-merger discussions.
2. **The Lone Wolf**. This is the sole owner and decision maker. They can be individuals looking to grow or eyeing succession. In some cases, sharing control of something they've built from the ground up can be challenging, or you may encounter the opposite—an owner who's completely ready to give up control and walk away.
3. **The Champion**. Protecting your client experience is key during an M&A event. This person, sometimes referred to as the Client Voice, is usually client-facing, potentially in a leadership role and has deep knowledge of the client experience.
4. **The Specialist**. With M&A becoming more and more prevalent with advisors, some firms now have someone on staff dedicated in some capacity to business development.
5. **The Tech**. It makes sense that during a technology integration, your staff IT or an outsourced IT professional is included in some of the strategy and assessment. This person will work with his/her counterpart in the other firm to develop a realistic plan of integration and implementation.

Wildcards: Expecting the Unexpected

The path to integration is not without its obstacles—some you see coming a mile away and others that T-bone you at an intersection at full speed. While you think you may be prepared for everything, the unique nature of each deal (and each firm), is bound to throw a few curveballs along the journey. Shaun and I call these "wild cards," and though they can happen at any stage during the transition, it's important to be aware of them right from the beginning. Here are a few to be aware of as you navigate your roadmap.

Good, Old Fashioned Human Nature

Many advisors began our careers as small business owners and entrepreneurs who started out in this industry to serve a greater purpose. We built our firms the hard way, from the ground up, starting from a small network of friends and family before seeing real growth throughout the years. We nurtured and protected our business, cultivated it carefully, adding good, solid people along the way who shared our passion for service and innovation. All of that care and investment naturally leads to a sense of ownership, pride, and yes, emotional attachment.

Those emotions are expected—from owners to advisors and the client service team—but you never know how they'll manifest themselves. Why? Because no amount of psychology can predict how individual people react and respond to immense change. During a merger or acquisition, you will be asking people to be very open-minded as some will need to relinquish control to do what's best for the larger firm. There will be a lot of questions that, if you're not careful, can start to sound like an interrogation.

Remember as you proceed to enter each interaction with empathy. Clearly communicate the purpose of your role (to bring everyone through this process successfully) and then engage in active listening. Be open to hearing different perspectives and acknowledging their immediate concerns. Even at this initial stage, seek to ease their fears all while anticipating upcoming changes and articulate how important each person will be as the process moves forward. There will be a tremendous desire by employees to hear details about key decisions—roles and responsibilities, which systems will be used, and much more—and you will not be able to provide these until later. This alone creates a great deal of uncertainty and anxiety for staff and being reassuring goes a long way.

Short-Sightedness

During all stages of your technology integration, I assure you there will be decisions along the way that seem to be low-hanging fruit. Easy decisions to check off a list and move on to the bigger items at hand. Always begin with your long-term strategy in mind. Making knee-jerk, tactical short-term decisions don't solve for the big picture.

For example, our IT team was hoping to make a quick decision about how to merge emails with a firm we acquired. I was given two options to consider to set up our email system—one would be a much shorter time commitment but would also be uniquely configured for this particular firm's current system. The second option was more involved and required an impact to the entire firm's email systems. Rather than decide quickly, I asked for more information. Which option would make it easier to repeat this exact process if we acquired another firm? Or two? Which option might be better suited for where we were going (vs. where we are right now)? The right answer meant more time up front today, but a lot less time in the future. Whenever possible, set yourself up for future success.

Subsets and Silos

It's not unusual for subsets of people in a firm to use technology differently. It would be no surprise to learn the operations team, advisors, and planning team all use technology in separate ways, especially once you start spending time with individual users. In fact, it's common for this to happen when there are multiple offices or departments within one larger firm. They may even be using different applications in different situations! The main question to ask in this situation is if the technology usage is consistent within the subgroupings across the firm. If it's not, find out what they are doing and why.

Mavericks

As soon as possible, identify individuals who tend to work their own way. These "individual contributors" or "rogue" team members who consistently do their own thing, without regard to strategy or systems, are potential dissenters you want to be aware of early on. It's not the end of the world to have mavericks but begin thinking about a plan for how to corral their independent nature.

Toxic Employees

Unfortunately, not everyone is suited for your newly merged firm. These are typically people who had behavior issues in their existing environment and have been allowed to continue acting poorly. During an M&A and changing conditions, this can cause even greater problems than they are already causing. These "toxic" employees might be disruptive, negative, contrary or information hoarders, and can affect your team's attitude and impact your forward momentum. It's important during the strategy phase to perform an evaluation of each team member as they fit into the new environment. What may have worked before needs to be redefined for the new firm.

Distractions, Delays and Discouragement

The three deadly "D's" can take away your focus and slow down momentum if left unchecked. These can include anything from high-priority initiatives in progress, market disruptions, and even the normal course of business every day. When merging systems, for example, it's hard to account for the daily issues that may already exist and require regular troubleshooting. There's a natural friction between the delivering service day-to-day and what the front-line client service people and advisors need to accomplish in their jobs. Migrating systems currently in heavy use essentially gets in the way of that and the impact can be seen as a hindrance, take "too long" to fix and slow down productivity.

Flexibility

You may have a very clear vision of where you want to go, but you never know when opportunities may pop up in the tech integration process. Those opportunities may not alter the big picture, but it can impact your strategy and your timeline. For example, during our last integration, I realized we needed to be building further forward faster with our IT. With two offices, we had planned to do a hybrid cloud desktop and eventually move to 100% virtual desktop. After some struggles, I realized we needed to go to 100% virtual desktop at launch, and we needed to get there fast. This decision did impact our timeline but looking forward with future acquisitions we'll be able to skip full steps.

Capacity

Most firms operate with the team they need to accomplish their goals. I don't know of anyone who has "extra" resources available on staff, and during a merger or acquisition, everyone needs to invest time beyond their existing duties to contribute to integration efforts. When your team is already operating at 80% capacity every day and suddenly handed large projects on a deadline, you're facing stress and burnout. Consider how you want to approach these projects ahead of time and communicate with the people you would expect to be involved. There may be a need for extra hands, overtime pay, or additional time factored into the timeline.

There Are No Shortcuts

Even for someone who is a technology enthusiast, I've made some mistakes that should have been caught earlier in the M&A process. For example, you can think that you're getting a shortcut if you find a firm that uses some of the same systems as yours—but you'll discover that *how* you use technology and *why* you use it can vary wildly from the other firm. It can also uncover a much bigger issue—one you never saw coming that could significantly impact your timeline.

During one of our acquisitions, we were thrilled to learn that both firms used the same CRM system. And as a bonus, we both utilized the same workflow functionality extensively. While this was fantastic news, we were unprepared for all of the varying factors that wouldn't make centralizing these workflows a snap. Most notably, Private Ocean was much larger than the other firm and our workflows had steps assigned to various people. On the other side, one person was completing multiple steps and, in some cases, condensing some important steps to save time. So, we arrived at an obstacle that could not easily be solved without reviewing our existing process and seeing how we might adapt it to work for both offices.

Larger firms often have more established processes and dedicated team members in certain roles. Attempting to centralize one aspect of our operations impacted job roles which meant we had a larger issue to address. In this situation, we realized that we started a bit backward. We were trying to integrate a system without the right people in the right roles in place. We learned that no matter how deceiving the shortcut, you can't start with technology—you have to start with your overall goals. In this case, our goal was to centralize some of this work. From there we should have assessed, integrated, and adapted our technology to work for us in this unique environment.

Key Takeaways

- Establish your end goals for the technology integration so that they align them with your overall firm goals. Ask:

  - Who are the decision makers at each firm related to technology?
  - What standards are in place today and what do exceptions look like?
  - Will you be taking the best of both worlds or is the acquiring firm the standard?

- In what direction are we headed as a combined entity?
- Be sensitive—Especially in this first stage, remember that everyone responds differently (and sometimes emotionally) to new processes and technology.
- Learn. The strategy of the operations team is to learn about the existing people, processes and technology by asking a series of important questions to gain an understanding about each firm's current perspectives.
- Change doesn't happen overnight and often is met with resistance, so communicate plans early.

Greg's Final Word

Setting yourself up for success during the strategy phase is crucial to a streamlined technology integration. How you approach and plan for this key part of your merger or acquisition sets the tone for every stage to come. Take a deep breath, slow down and even take a step back if needed. Start with creating a big picture of where you're trying to go and remember that communication, patience, and collaboration are key. You don't need to have all the answers, but you should have a clear vision of your future. I can tell you that with Private Ocean, I can always see our next destination. I have a mental picture of the client experience and the technology that we'll need to get there. But it's not a vision created in a vacuum—I have an idea but I am always open to changing how we get there. Keep an open mind and welcome all the ideas from your team, your consultants, and your peers.

3

Setting Your Integration Timeline

Once you've performed an initial assessment of your people, processes, and technology and developed a strategy, it's time to lay out a projected roadmap for execution. The reason I say "projected" is that you don't know all that you need to know to do a 100% accurate timeline—there will likely be adjustments necessary. However, a timeline for integration should be addressed early on, ideally, right on the heels of strategy. Once you know your tentative date for the deal to close you can begin your discovery. As you near the closing date you want to begin planning to integrate and implement your technology strategy. A good point of reference, from my experience, is to expect each project (whether it's integrating your CRM, implementing a new financial planning system or relaunching a website) to take somewhere between three to six months to fully complete. Between assessments, dependencies, and corresponding activities—not to mention continuing to run your business—you should anticipate each stage taking some time and finesse to get right.

In this chapter, Shaun and I will offer our shared approach on the stages of a technology integration timeline, and we'll each provide our insight and experience from a leadership and operations perspective during this key phase.

© The Author(s) 2018
G. Friedman and S. Kapusinski, *The Financial Advisor M&A Guidebook*,
https://doi.org/10.1007/978-3-030-00003-5_3

Leading the Charge

From a leadership perspective, you should develop a clear picture of "success"—in other words, what the combined entity looks like from a systems and operations perspective in a highly efficient and effective state. As the decision maker (or makers), it's up to you to communicate those goals and create clear targets that get you there. And because your operations people are the ones planning for and performing the actual tactics needed for strategy execution, it's ideal to have operations involved as soon as possible. For the operations manager, it's their job to assess what needs to be accomplished and prioritize actions based on the reality of your timeline.

To start planning, let's first talk about important events in the process.

Events to Help Shape Your Timeline

- *Initial Talks*: Let's set expectations here. There is no set time for how long this stage can take, and in our experience it can take months. Usually, there isn't much detail unveiled to too many people on either side of the table. Often, it's very hush-hush outside of those closest to the deal itself since these conversations can take quite a while to pan out. From a discovery standpoint you are generally only learning at the highest levels what the major systems and processes are but not a lot of detail (such as HOW these systems are being used).
- *Letter of Intent (LOI)*: Often a letter of intent is signed once the parties have gone through initial talks and have agreed to move forward toward a deal (a formal purchase agreement). This is likely to kick off a heavy due diligence period. Much of what needs to take place leading up to this event and during due diligence is covered in the next chapter.
- *Soft Close*: Once the legal work is completed, it's considered a "soft close." This is the date where the purchase or merger agreements are signed, followed by a public announcement once the firms are ready with a marketing plan. At this point, there is a lot of work to do to finalize the deal, such as client notifications, potentially new client agreements and custodial paperwork, and hopefully some systems and procedures integration. This event can certainly be the green light for beginning implementation (covered in Chapter 5). Please note that all deals may

have different timing based on many factors such as the client agreements in place, goals of the firms, etc.

- *Hard Close or "Day 1"*: This is the date when client agreements are being updated with the new RIA and you begin to operate internally and externally as one firm.

With these "mile markers" in mind, consider these benchmarks in the integration process to estimate how much time you'll need to complete each phase. Speaking from experience, you should never box yourself in to a hard deadline—be flexible and always factor in possible delays and obstacles that may result in moving timelines.

Six Key Milestones of Tech Integration

- *Initial Assessment*: During the initial talks, both parties usually reveal a high-level summary of the types of systems they use, their workflows, and the processes. At this point, you don't want to invest a ton of time, but you do start looking under the hood at basic systems and infrastructure. It will give you an idea of how the two firms can work together.
- *Deeper Dive and Due Diligence*: This typically starts after you sign the LOI and continues all the way through final implementation and execution. At this point, you'll start digging into the systems used by each firm and assessing people, capacity, and efficiency. Some questions you'll want to cover in this stage: *Where are your opportunities and red flags? Are there dormant systems that go unused? Are the current systems being used properly and consistently? Are there power users in the firm? What integrations are being used?*
- *Setting a Preliminary Plan and Strategy*: Next, you'll map out your strategy and envision how your combined firm will operate. At the end of this stage, you'll know which systems you want to keep and use. You'll then work with operations, IT and other teams to develop a realistic timeline for implementation of each system.
- *Kick off and Implementation*: Create a macro plan as far as timing based on your firm's model. *Will the two firms continue to function separately or merge into one brand? Will you have satellite offices or remote employees? Are there functions you will centralize (such as portfolio trading)?*

Whatever your infrastructure, each integration should align with your overall plan. For example, at Private Ocean, our last acquisition resulted in two offices with the intention of everyone following the same workflows using the same systems. We followed this sequence (however some of these were being worked on at the same time) based on the firm's strategy:

1. **CRM integration**. We focused on completing this integration first as we considered this the "domino" in our tech suite that centralized our workflows.
2. **Portfolio accounting and trading systems**. Next, we wanted to centralize operations and begin aligning people in the right roles.
3. **IT integration**. Simultaneously, we kicked off email, calendar and phone integration efforts as different people were responsible for this technology and we could spread out resources.
4. **Portals and website**. We then engaged marketing to sweep through existing collateral to integrate the new firm and create a seamless online experience for clients.

- *Internal Training*: Once you've migrated data and implemented the systems, be sure to schedule ample time for teams to learn how to use new or merged technology and processes.
- *Launch or "Day 1"*: This is essentially when you decide to begin fully using new or merged technology and following any newly combined processes. If applicable, you may also plan for an announcement to clients. As it relates to technology, many projects are internal and don't directly impact clients. For the changes that *do* impact clients (switching portals, for instance), this is the point when you'd kick off your communication plan to let clients know a change is being made. You'll offer resources, training, and answer questions to ensure a smooth transition.

Putting It Together

Considering the various stages of the deal and planning your assessment and inventory accordingly, let's put the two together. Your timeline should look something like this image below:

The Six Key Milestones of Technology Integration

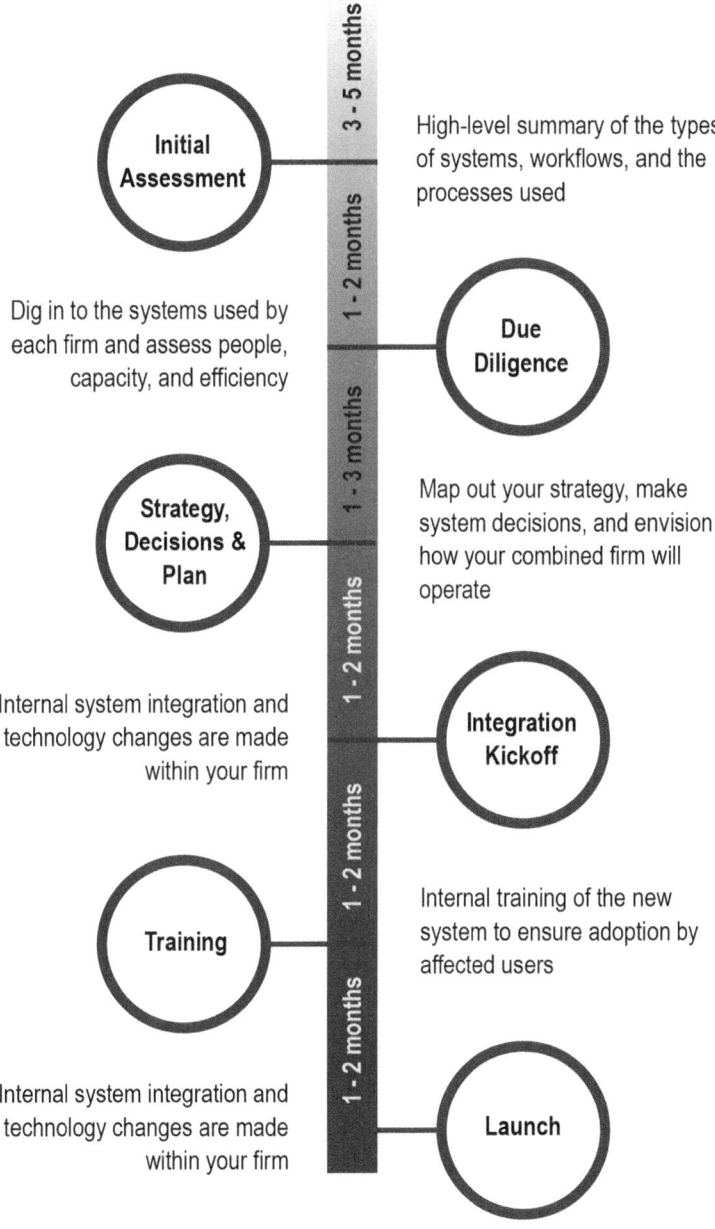

Obviously, every M&A transaction is unique and various factors will impact your technology integration. You may want to implement a cyclical timeline and break up your integration into smaller chunks. Based on what you need and where you want to go, draft a timeline that is both realistic and aligns with your overall strategy. Shaun explains in this next section why timing matters—and what you should be aware of as you go into planning for this stage.

Why Timing Matters

My older sister was a competitive swimmer in high school. She, along with her teammates, trained hard before and after school, swimming lap after lap, putting in the necessary time, and effort to be in top condition for their meets. One of her events was the relay, in which four swimmers take turns covering the same distance in the pool.

To avoid disqualification in a relay, you must wait until the previous swimmer touches the side of the pool before leaving its edge. So during practices, when the four swimmers came together to practice for the relay, they didn't focus on the swimming (since their training prepared them for that part already)—but instead, their time together focused on the exchanges. My sister would wait until she saw her teammate finish, and then dive in.

But after a few meets, her coach began to work with her on winding up—a practice where the upcoming swimmer begins their jump before the other swimmer has finished. It can be tricky, but if one swimmer can start moving at the same time toward the same end goal as the other swimmer, and as long as the previous swimmer's hand touches the side before the other's feet are in the air, it's a qualified exchange. And since swimming is a sport where timing matters, it's a practice that's highly encouraged.

The same idea of people moving at the same time toward the same goal is true for the timing of operations during a merger or acquisition. Some people will need to finish their work but others can get ready to move in the meantime.

No matter what angle you want to come at it, prioritizing is key. Having more time allows you the opportunity for more choices, whereas a shorter timeline will only allow you to make decisions on little more than just the essentials. Know that preparing for a transition will look remarkably different if you have 3 months or less, versus 6–9 months to prepare.

That being said, many transitions happen over 3–9 months. Some can be very quick (3 months or less) and occasionally there are those with a timeline of over 9 months—which can feel like a luxury.

Two Steps Back, One Step Forward

When setting milestones, you shouldn't be overly aggressive with your goals and don't underestimate the time it will actually take to integrate. When Private Ocean made one of our acquisitions, for example, our goal was to consolidate investment operations. We estimated a conservative time investment to complete this transition but uncovered a giant curveball with the firm's database and vendor that turned the project into something we knew would take much more time than we first anticipated—and we were concerned about our team's capacity to complete the project without putting other work on hold. Some advisors may be tempted to insist on the team moving forward no matter the impact. But we took this opportunity to learn that next time we needed to be more rigorous in our due diligence up front and we needed to be extra sensitive to how people work and how their work affects our clients. Tough decisions still needed to be made, but we took two steps back in this case before we could move one step forward.

Key Takeaways

- Be realistic about your timeline. Every transition is different—don't get caught up in comparing your event to any other firms', not even your past experiences.
- Start with a macro plan for your timeline that aligns with the firm's overall goals, then create micro project plans for each system.
- Foster open communication! If your people don't have enough resources, don't feel like a deadline is realistic, or if the team is under stress, whatever the situation, be sure to communicate to your team that they need to speak up. As a leader, it's your job to remove obstacles and offer guidance that empowers your people to achieve their goals.
- Never box yourself into a drop-dead date for completing an integration—always factor in possible delays and obstacles that may result in moving timelines.
- Every decision you make is for the greater good of the firm and its clients—not what's most convenient or easy to accomplish in the shortest amount of time. I often tell my team that the first 12 months after an M&A event is focusing on getting your legs under you, and year two is about growth.

Greg's Final Word

Setting a timeline is an incredibly useful tool to help communicate the firm's goals to everyone on the team. From the time you start negotiations, to closing, to setting goals beyond the initial integration, it shows an intentional growth and keeps everyone motivated and on the same path.

If you're feeling overwhelmed at the prospect of setting a timeline, just remember it's okay not to have all the details at the start. No one does, really, and it's through your assessment and due diligence that you'll uncover things along the way that need to be considered. Just think of setting your overall timeline like seating an orchestra for a symphony. Who needs to sit in front? Who should have the solos? Who supports the brass section? Is everyone practicing the same tune? How you prepare in advance of your technology launch date makes the difference between sounding like an 8th grade band of recorders and the New York Philharmonic. Remember, your clients are the audience, and ultimately, you want them to be satisfied and delighted with the outcome.

4

Inventory and Assessment: How Your Technology Stacks Up

As we discussed in Chapter 2, the assessment and due diligence stage of technology integration should be treated as its own project, with a timeline and scope taken into consideration. In this chapter, I'll offer my perspective on this key step from a leadership perspective, then Shaun will walk us through his approach to creating an inventory of technology and data, assessing technology use across both firms, and anticipating the impact of both internal and external changes.

The overarching themes for this stage are: (1) patience, and (2) making sure the right people are involved. As time is always in limited supply, the inventory and assessment stage of integration is an area where we've experienced some impatience amongst firms. After all, how long does it *really* take to make a list of technology systems, decide which ones to keep, and merge them already?

The answer: longer than you think if you want it done right. If you make mistakes at this stage, the cost of any bad shortcuts, workarounds, poor implementations, missteps, and miscommunication is very high. The energy you're going to put out and the time you're going to waste is considerable. So, flip your thinking. Take your time and patience to invest—because you either do it on the front end or you potentially pay a big price on the back end.

© The Author(s) 2018
G. Friedman and S. Kapusinski, *The Financial Advisor M&A Guidebook*,
https://doi.org/10.1007/978-3-030-00003-5_4

How Involved Should You Be?

As a leader, you need to decide from the start how and at what level you want to be involved in this stage of the process. Speaking for myself, as someone who tries to maximize technology use, I like to be kept involved but I'm also realistic about time constraints. That's why I enlist people I trust to do the heavy lifting on the front end. Once a full assessment is done, this group—often led by operations—presents their findings for leadership to review.

Where you should contribute is on the front end of the process. There is a certain amount of self-reflection and business-reflection that happens during this stage, no matter how many times you have gone through the M&A process. The type of questions you should be asking about your technology include, "Is your current technology fitting the needs and goals of your business?" "Does your technology serve the needs of your clients the way you want it to?" "How well does your team utilize your tools?" "Are they effective?" "Are you monitoring business metrics to keep track of the efficiency of your business?" Some of the answers to those questions might be difficult to swallow, but it's an excellent time to address any issues you identify. Why? Because you're already asking these questions of the other firm. Where are the opportunities? What's going well and what needs work? What issues are we trying to solve for today?

From there, you'll start to expand the circle and start identifying team leads and/or the right people who can assist operations in the actual inventory and assessment (Shaun will go into this in more detail later in this chapter). At Private Ocean we have a Tech Committee, and someone from every area of the firm is represented.

Don't forget that everybody is a player on the board, including your clients. Don't be afraid to ask for initial input on a wider scale. All of this information helps to identify the areas where you want operations to hone in. Do clients wish the firm had an app? Do they like the current portal? Do team members find the existing process for onboarding easy and efficient? Does anyone have an issue with their computer systems, their email or their phones? No question is out of scope and being proactive only encourages people to share their current experience.

Last but not least, whether you have two people or 20 people involved, it helps to keep things organized for leadership using a project management tool. There is a definite need to track and monitor progress and offer transparency across both firms. There are a variety of these tools to choose from, so we suggest doing your research to find one that best suits your needs.

Now that you're armed with data, feedback, opportunities, and an organizational system, it's time to move forward to start the inventory, assessment, and due diligence phase of the integration process. Shaun will walk us through his approach for completing this stage, including the impact of change during the process.

Operations at the Helm

From an operations leader's perspective, it's after an LOI is signed when you will be more heavily involved in the integration process if you haven't been already. As we prefaced in Chapter 2, hopefully, you've already been brought in and have an idea of the acquired firm's major systems used, the custodian(s) involved, and any unique ways the new firm operates differently from your firm. If you don't know anything about these areas yet, then this is your starting point.

Who's Involved?

The owners or leaders of the M&A negotiations will drive the decision for when a task force is ready to be organized. But by the time an LOI is signed, the lead firm often already has a select team in place. This top-level team probably met in person to start laying out a plan before the specifics of the deal had even been drafted. Once an LOI is signed though, it's time for you to get involved and start moving.

It's a given that there will be ongoing participation from the owners and other personnel who were involved in the making of the deal. Beyond this, you'll want to consider forming an integration team. It is possible that this group will form naturally, but if not, you want to include those individuals with leadership roles in different areas of the firm that will be impacted by the merger or acquisition.

Key members of the integration team should be leadership from the following areas of your firm (which may be a few people wearing multiple hats, depending on the type and size of your firm):

- Owners, or the business team focused on the specifics of the agreement itself
- Key senior advisors (or a representative)
- Compliance personnel

- Technology officers
- Operations: including Client Service, Custodian relations, and Investment Management which will include trading and reporting
- The Financial Planning team
- Marketing
- Human Resources

You may find reasons to pull in even more people depending on your strategy but having representatives from the above groups should cover all areas of the firm's technology and integration needs as you move forward.

An Outside Perspective

As soon as feasibly possible, start to involve the relevant custodians, software vendors, and anyone else that may be involved from a technology perspective. It behooves you to give your important vendor relationships notice about a deal that will likely take some of their time and attention in the near future.

It's a good idea to ask custodians about key information they will be wanting from your firm and if there will be any potential costs that you may incur when the deal goes through. If the expenses will be significant and depending on who may be doing the work (internal versus hired), these costs may even play into the strategic decisions around the purchase price if an acquisition is being made.

Custodians are an extension of your technology; we all interface with their websites, our portfolio systems need their data, and even CRM systems may be integrated. In this case, you might naturally start to openly discuss the specifics of integrating the two firms together early on.

Major software system vendors, especially those you'll have to migrate data for, will also be high on the list to begin discussions with as early as possible. Let them know what is going on and how you may need their services at some point soon. Welcome their suggestions and guidance related to new data coming into their particular system.

Third parties are also an option during this diagnostic phase if you're looking for an objective opinion on vetting technology. The only caveat is that you shouldn't rely on any one source, and you shouldn't be passive if you do engage outside opinions to help select technology. You still have to do your homework.

Creating an Inventory

In an ideal world, you'd have as much time as you want to get all the information you need to make the right decisions at every turn. But that's not realistic. What *is* realistic is getting your mind around each piece of technology being used at the firm and using that inventory to prioritize within your actual time frame.

To get started, look to your operations team leaders to work together on developing a plan for gathering information about the technology and data components of both firms. It's important to know what are the must-haves for Day 1, what would be nice-to-have, and what can wait.

Keep in mind, the pace can sometimes make you feel like you don't have enough time. That's normal. But it's your responsibility to make the things under your control—things that need to happen—happen. This is also why it's so important to have operations involved early. When you're at the table with the decision makers, you can give important insight as to what can actually be done in the time frame for which they're planning.

Project Planning

Like Greg mentioned at the beginning of the chapter, a merger or acquisition is a big project—treat it like one. It deserves the weight of your attention and priority of your time. Before you start, decide on a way to keep track of everything. Also, have a plan for communication to your key team players, including leadership. Use whatever medium that works best for you and your situation.

Routine meetings, emails, posts, visuals and/or personal messaging software are all helpful and recommended ways of keeping everyone in the loop. Recurring status updates on key areas are important to keep major players on the same page with what is happening—and with what needs to happen. Plus, frequent updates will help show your progress, which is a great motivator for upcoming and ongoing tasks needing to be completed.

As Greg mentioned, there are numerous project management tools available. Do you have to have one? No. Are they helpful? Absolutely. Many tools today provide sufficient transparency to cut down on the need for emails or other manual communications. It's worth using a cloud-based application for easily shared access, especially with your new teammates, who are likely at another location. This tool will be extremely helpful for a team who is not yet sharing any network drives.

Taking an Inventory

In order to take inventory, you need to break the firm's major systems into parts. Listed below are the main categories and major systems of many RIA firms.[1]

- Software

  - Customer Relationship Management (CRM)
  - Portfolio management
  - Trading and rebalancing
  - Financial planning
  - Billing
  - Accounting
  - Document management
  - Risk analysis
  - Forms management
  - Compliance/cybersecurity
  - Security: email encryption, device management
  - Client vault/portal
  - Research and analytics
  - Basic productivity software for email, documents, spreadsheets, etc.

- Hardware

  - Servers (on-site or not)
  - Phones (hard/soft)
  - Desktops/laptops
  - Mobile devices
  - Printers/scanners/copiers/faxes
  - Security systems/cameras

- Ancillary

  - Digital planning or investment solutions
  - Digital signature tools
  - Web conferencing tools
  - Expense management

---

[1]Drucker, D., and Bruckenstein, J. (2012) *Technology Tools for Today's High-Margin Practice: How Client-Centered Financial Advisors Can Cut Paperwork, Overhead, and Wasted Hours*. Bloomberg Press, New York, Partial List.

- Automated calendaring
- Company's website
- Learning management system for training
- Conference call provider
- Dictation service
- Aggregation software
- Cloud storage
- Instant messaging
- Virtual private network access

For each of these systems, seek out the vital information. How is it used? By whom? What data is important? Is it a must-have or a nice-to-have for Day 1?

One of the biggest concerns while taking inventory is missing a software system or vital piece of information. It's not unusual for people to fail to see a gap or have a blind spot with systems. In order to avoid this, seek to talk to the actual users, not just those in charge. Ask a lot of questions about what might be missing in their daily usage and always ask about exceptions—what's unique or different? What haven't we asked you about that you use every day—or even occasionally? It is also important to ask what's currently working well for them, and what isn't or could be improved.

To have this much detail early will set you up for a robust action plan. But don't be discouraged if you find out little more than what software is being used before you begin taking an inventory—simply because of timing. This is common. For many acquisitions, it's after the LOI is signed and all employees are aware of what's happening that you will have better access and be able to begin to gather all the vital information on these systems.

Assessing the Technology

Now that you have an idea of what technology exists, it's time to start your assessment. Many of you will already be thinking along these lines or started working on this step while you were taking inventory.

Make an Outline

Strengths/Weaknesses
It can be helpful to use an outline to see every system you need to evaluate. Start by lining up each category of systems. Then, assess the strong and weak points of each on the list. Strong points often are reasons why current users

like working with the system, what clients enjoy about it, and generally, why it works well for the firm. Weak points are areas where the system frustrates your team, what your clients wish for, and what the vendor says they'll build "someday."

Special Considerations

- Legacy systems: Are they deeply entrenched? Will they be messy to migrate?
- What are the client facing impacts of each system?
- Contracts/agreements: Will there be costly exit fees?
- Existing projects: Will changes have an immediate negative impact on work in process?
- Integrations: If it's on your technology roadmap or a strategic goal, consider the potential for current and future integration.
- Upgrades/enhancements: Is the program out of date? When was it last updated? Has it ever been updated? Is it cloud-based? Does it have heavy maintenance?
- Future of vendor: In what direction is each vendor headed? Are they a tech dinosaur? Do they heavily invest in enhancements? Have they themselves been acquired recently and has that change led to better or worse service and offerings?
- Price: Is it a "great system" only because it meets your cost requirements? Is there value for the price? Is there a reason to justify an overlap of systems, in light of the price?
- Essential: Is this system necessary for what you want to accomplish? Is this brand a must? Could the requirements be met by other systems in the same category?

Timing

You want to consider which systems are the most important to each firm. One of the questions you need to answer is if the systems will change when you become a combined entity. At this point, you know your timeframe and are beginning to think from short term to long term.

In the short term, or now till the deal's hard close, decide what systems must be in place for operations to continue on Day 1. In light of your time frame, these will be your must-haves.

Consider anything that needs to be done within the first year a medium-term priority. Set goals for what can be accomplished after the hard close.

Table 4.1 Systems assessment

System list by category	Pros/strengths/ clients love/ team values	Cons/weaknesses/ frustrations/gaps/ risks	Special considerations	Timing/ urgency/ importance
CRM Product A Product B				
Portfolio management software Product C Product D				
Planning software Product E Product F Product G				

Long-term, or any time past the first anniversary of the hard close, system goals may include inventory items that were on your "what can wait" list. This may include consolidation or integration of systems to large decisions which take into consideration the clients' and firm's best interests for the future. Some examples of long-term goals are online portals, document management systems, or upgraded portfolio management systems.

Ask the Tough Questions
Once you see the systems together in one place, look at your list critically for gaps, blind spots, and risks. Then begin asking critical questions:

- Is there overlap?
- What can stay?
- What needs to go?
- Whose checklist will we use?
- Do we agree on which systems are critical?

An example of this assessment is provided in Table 4.1.

A Step Past Tech

Assessing the technology should also include reaching beyond the systems themselves. You need to look at the processes. It's important to know what each system is capable of, not just what it's currently used for. You want to know what it does for your firm and for the clients—who benefits the most? The least? Not at all? Spend some time discussing how you're going to address any differences of process. And then, in light of the timeline, will those differences be addressed in the short term, medium term, or long term?

As we mentioned earlier, talk to the users of each system. Ask to speak with those who use the existing systems day in and day out. Determine which teams or departments and individual users utilize the technology. Evaluate the team dynamics. Is usage mandatory or encouraged? Forced or enjoyed? Are notes added into the CRM because it's helpful for service or because people are told to do so? Or are notes not added at all?

At every level, get an understanding of who does what, and where any exceptions exist. Find out if all advisors use the portfolio management system. Do only a few team members track birth dates in your CRM? Is it acceptable for certain advisors not to use the financial planning software for client projections? You want to have as clear of a picture as possible of what is actually happening, not just what's supposed to be happening related to all aspects of technology.

Reality Check

Spencer Segal, CEO of ActiFi, speaks at conferences about Level 5 firms— firms where everything is automated through data within highly integrated software systems. Not only is everything a process, but it's an automated one; systems communicate with one another and people aren't bogged down by monotonous activities.

Let's be clear: many of us have a long way to go before we'd be considered a Level 5 firm.

So be honest with where you are. There's no benefit in selling yourself as something you're not. Both sides of an M&A transaction will benefit by being open, forthright, and transparent as it relates to the use, benefits, adoption, and value provided by each piece of technology being assessed.

Change Management During Assessment

Part of your planning phase is preparing for the change to come. Change for organizations is complex and creates uncertainty and even anxiety for some people. When firms aren't used to any regular growth changes or technology enhancements, needing to make big modifications can feel overwhelming to do all at once. Yet to a firm that has been growing and is accustomed to implementing new processes or updating current practices regularly, the prospect of an impending transition won't be met with the same amount of resistance.

In Bob Veres' book, *The New Profession*, he talks about how our openness to change does not come naturally. In fact, we resist it. Resisting change doesn't serve us well, yet most everyone wants to stay where they are. Yet after change happens, especially in the growth of a firm looking to make improvements across the line for everyone involved, no one wants to return to how it was before, either.[2]

Don't lose sight of the challenges inherent to change, nor take its effects lightly. It is a big deal to go through this event, especially for the firm being acquired or merging in. Many employees experience worry and anxiety over questions like: Where do I fit? What is my future? Will I be valued here as I was before? What will be the impact on my job, my role, and even how the new management will view my performance?

Questions about the unknown, as well as a loss of control, are normal, and we can't underestimate the impact this event may have on members of the team. I always counsel people that it serves you well to view change as a GOOD thing and not immediately worry about negative consequences of change.

So how do you deal with the challenges of change that inherently come with migrating not only culture, but systems, software, and procedures?

1. **Don't rush to get everything done.**
   Your focus needs to be on Day 1 priorities, such as transitioning accounts as needed. Some software, systems, and procedures will need to be ready at that point, but not everything in your inventory list will. It's acceptable to set out a schedule that works for everyone involved, from your internal team to the clients.
2. **Deal with your exceptions and foreseeable issues early.**
   Some examples of potential trouble spots: if all passwords are on one spreadsheet; you rely upon a single person for daily reconciliation or an approval process and if that server is on its last leg. The sooner you can get these issues onto the table (and, better yet, there with some potential solutions), the easier it will be for everyone to accept the change when it comes.

---

[2]Veres, B. (2016) *The New Profession*. Independent Publisher, p. 22.

3. **Limit the technological disruptions.**

   In order to help both staff and clients, make as minimal as possible changes to the technology being used. Change isn't only happening to the people within the firm—clients also undergo change during this process. You want your team to focus on the clients and smooth out their transition too.

4. **Have a plan for dealing with pushback.**

   In some instances, there may be resistance. Buy-in from the top of both firms is key. With solid people management in place, it will be easier to lay a path for successful integration of both firms.

5. **Communicate often.**

   Communication is a vital part of this process. Use your existing meetings and personal connection time to help people talk through the upcoming changes. Give them opportunities to ask questions and express concerns. Be honest. Don't sugar coat the challenges coming but be encouraging about the end goals and the dedication to getting everyone to the end-point together. And most importantly, repeat over and over what's in it for them and the firm for accomplishing this work.

In a conversation I had with Nathan Mersereau, the President of Planning Alternatives in Bloomfield Hills, MI, he spoke to me about how he dealt with the pressure of change prior to the close of his largest merger.

He told me that when you're dealing with change management prior to the close of a deal, the message needs to be clear:

- *Things are changing and change is here to stay.* We are growing and it's part of who we are as a firm and who we will continue to be. Jack Welch said, "If the rate of change on the outside exceeds the rate of change on the inside, then the end is near." In essence, what he means is that we must undergo continual changes in order to survive as an entity.
- *I'm listening.* Through listening, your goal is to get buy-in. You want to hear all the voices on the team. Seek suggestions and guidance from team members that can be woven into the actual outcomes. When people are heard and involved, it makes an impact.
- *Here's what's coming next.* Communicate regularly and clearly. Keep your team members informed. Share milestones that have been met and what's coming up next. Communicate more than you think you should. Don't underestimate the value of an early heads-up for people undergoing a lot of change in a short amount of time.

Mersereau visualized the future by drawing this simple diagram to help everyone understand where they were headed:

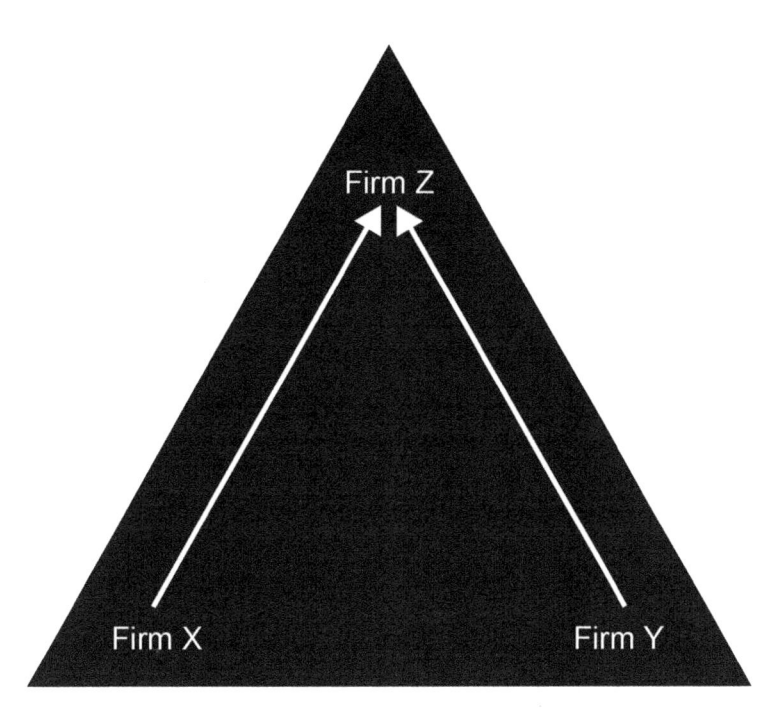

Combining firms X and Y into a new firm Z helps everyone see how the future is going to be full of change for everyone from both firms.

Throughout the entirety of this book, we want you to keep in mind the importance of culture and people within a firm. Yes, there will be technology to change, and processes to change, but without people who are willing to change, neither of the first two will be successful.

Wildcards: Avoiding the Snags

You're Short on Time

Not all deals will give you three or more months to prepare. So the main concern is to prioritize what needs to be done for Day 1. Some have argued that it's not worth cramming to get all of the important systems to go live on Day 1. And I agree. It's going to be okay to run dual systems for some time if it simply can't be done before your first day as one firm.

Your Counterparts Aren't Available Enough

As we discussed the burdens on the integration team, which will include parties from both sides, sometimes their capacity and availability do not line up. In those cases, there are a few things you can do:

1. Make it easy: have agendas for meetings, be concise with questions and don't waste any unnecessary time.
2. Look to help: find ways to make your counterparts' jobs easier or to get them support through delegation or alternatives.
3. Keep them informed: keep your new colleagues well aware of your progress in a communication method that's best for them. Ideally, you take advantage of a cloud-based project tracking system (mentioned earlier) to provide constant visibility.

Consider using additional outside resources to help during your transition project. These can be your vendors or industry consultants, or even temporary administrative help.

You Can't Come to an Agreement

It's certainly possible that even with deep assessments, comparisons, and conversations, two parties may not easily agree on a system or how a tool should be used. This shouldn't be viewed as adversarial—a me vs. you situation. It just means that two parties feel equally strong about their stance on the technology. In this instance, try involving a few outside people for their objective view. From there, it may go to leadership, keeping in mind always that the final decision is always designed with the best outcome for the firm and its clients in mind.

Key Takeaways

- The drivers of the deal need to have a plan to carry out the strategy behind where this M&A event will go.
- After there's an agreement (legal or not) you'll be able to start taking inventory during serious due diligence.
- Part of the assessment phase is asking questions about usage, norms, and expectations when it comes to each other's systems.

- Go beyond the technology itself to gain a better understanding of both the people using it (how it's used, why they use it, when they don't use it) and the processes they follow driving its utilization.
- Finally, we addressed that change can be challenging. You want to curb anxiety and fear without disrupting the flow of people doing their jobs. As you objectively assess what needs to be done, you'll also strive to be sensitive to people's needs—knowing that some will adapt faster and easier than others.
- Your plan for moving and merging systems and data starts by building out a mindset among the members of your team. Guide them, answer their "Why's," and give them a vision.

Greg's Final Word

The assessment stage of the integration process is time-consuming and takes effort, patience, and diplomacy. It's a delicate time when two parties are sharing how they use technology to serve their clients and the firm, and inevitably, everyone knows a change is coming. As a leader, you need to be sensitive to how this stage can affect your people and be sure to keep a pulse on the process if you're limited on how much you can be involved. Delegate but ask for progress updates. Know when things are lagging behind and jump in when needed. Be available for conversations and decisions. Be passionate about the end goal and communicate it often. Be hyper aware of the impact of change on people and culture. Most of all, expect that this stage will take time.

5

Getting Started with Implementation

You've compared notes, assessed, and researched the programs, and you've drafted your people into the integration process as team leads and team players. You have your goals and your milestones set and your strategy and timeline in place. You've completed all the necessary legwork, now it's time to get started executing on all of those plans.

Implementation is a very exciting step in the process as you'll begin to see the results of all your hard work. In this chapter, I'll kick things off with an outline of how leaders can help guide the integration and implementation process through communication and organization, then Shaun will share his approach to working with the different teams for execution.

Leadership Through Organization

My son is a classical musician and I've learned a lot from him about each role a different section of the orchestra plays to execute a complex piece of music. It's similar with each technology platform. Every system that needs to be integrated should have an assigned "conductor" who best understands the technology and is qualified and capable of leading the implementation process. This conductor, or the team lead, is someone who rolls up their sleeves and works with their colleagues while also communicating with project managers, operations, and management. The team lead is a vital part of the integration process, and Shaun will speak to their role during the implementation phase later in this chapter.

© The Author(s) 2018
G. Friedman and S. Kapusinski, *The Financial Advisor M&A Guidebook*,
https://doi.org/10.1007/978-3-030-00003-5_5

I firmly believe that sometimes the best thing a leader can do is get out of the way. If you've got the right people managing a project, there's no need to overmanage. Where leaders can make an impact is in clear communication, setting priorities, removing obstacles, and offering the right tools for organization that promotes transparency, accountability, and forward motion.

Project Management

Today it seems that there are more project management applications than there are people, but that shouldn't deter you from selecting a system that works best for your firm. These systems are designed to be intuitive, easy to use, and best of all, help your people organize all the milestones and tasks for your integration. Quick reports offer management a high-level overview of your progress without much effort, and project managers and operations can use this tool to check with team leads on outstanding items.

Where this becomes extremely helpful is in regular check-ins with teams. At Private Ocean, our project manager meets with the team leads before, during and after implementation for 15 minutes a week. These meetings are not intended to be rigid—rather they're an informal touch-point to see how the project is moving along and if any obstacles have popped up that need addressing by leadership.

This approach has both empowered our people to lead the charge while keeping management updated on the timeline and progress. Being removed a bit is a good thing in my opinion; it allows me to focus on how I can play my part in the process. On our regular monthly leadership calls, we can talk about the big picture. How are the various moving parts and priorities working for the team? Managing our implementation as individual projects this way has afforded us a solid amount of structure, clear accountability, and lots of flexibility.

Managing Timelines

From my experience, one of the biggest challenges of integrating technology is sticking to your timeline. While some leaders and principals have an idea of the scope, I consider those people to be the exception, not the rule. My background in technology—and running a fintech firm—has given me a tremendous appreciation for what goes into development, integration, implementation, and training. At Private Ocean and in the past at Junxure, I have relied heavily on my leaders to define the scope of a project, how long they anticipate that project taking to complete, and what kind of impact it will have on our staff. From there, I superimpose the needs and goals of the business, i.e., "In 12 months we should be here," or "By the end of the year we need to achieve this."

Working toward realistic goals is motivating and gives people something to budget toward time-wise. But you also have to factor into that a few things. First, the natural rhythm of the business. You don't jump into an integration project in December, for instance, or start assessing your technology in the middle of tax season.

Now, it's safe to assume that most of your designated team leads are not sitting around waiting for you to find them an M&A project. It's your responsibility in management to both understand the needs of the business and be keenly aware of what everyone is working on. Open communication is key to planning the who, what, where, how, and when of an integration.

The second factor that could impact timing during this stage is how much disruption you're willing to absorb to get the job done. At Private Ocean our guiding principles are at the core of everything we do—including beginning integration projects. Our guiding principles are:

Everything we do is in service of our clients.
Our words are our commitments.
We pursue excellence in all things.
We are intellectually curious.
Everyone has an important contribution.
Life is short. Laugh.

The types of questions we ask—how will this process disrupt client services in the short term? What is our communication strategy both internally and externally? How can we continue to provide excellent care during this time?

Taking these things as they come—you can only plan so much and there are always curve balls—your options as a leader are to decide how your timeline might move, the impacts on staff and clients, if more resources are needed, or if you need to consider an alternate route to implementation. It really does depend on the situation but understanding these common roadblocks can be helpful in preparing a game plan to head off any major delays. With that said it is important to be flexible—"life" happens!

There Are No Perfect Recipes

A question that Shaun and I hear often from advisors has to do with documenting. As in, "Can we capture this process and repeat it in the event of another M&A event?" The answer is yes, but with a big caveat.

Every M&A deal is different on so many levels that it's difficult to create a formula for success. What worked well last time might not apply the next time. The size of the firm, the resources available, the type of technology used, and the details and structure of the deal itself all create a completely unique situation that can't be replicated exactly.

What is consistent is that you know what areas you'll be addressing. From compliance to asset management to legal, marketing, operations, and wealth planning, there will always be the same key areas where you'll need to perform due diligence. And even though the experience may be different each time, you should have a clear idea what you'd like to understand and achieve within each segment.

Just keep in mind that this is not a science. There is no exact formula. Rather than document processes with the intent of repeating them, we recommend a different approach. Consider lessons learned—what went well and not so well last time? How can you be better prepared for each phase (strategy, due diligence, data gathering, goal setting, etc.) so that you can be more efficient and ask better questions? It's less about creating a Standard Operating Procedure (SOP) playbook, and more about focusing on the bigger picture today and where you want to be headed tomorrow.

Now it's time to get started. Shaun will guide us through his process for working with the team toward a successful implementation.

Jumping In, Feet First

Up to this point, you've been building your project plan through the questions you've asked and the cache of information you've gathered as a result. Now that you know what you're working with, it's time to start putting together the outline of your game plan and identifying your top priorities. It may feel like a big step, but if you've done the work identified in the previous chapters, the jump from planning to implementation should be seamless.

For those of you who have already been involved in the strategy and planning phases, be prepared for an even larger time investment now. If you're a key operations or integration manager, this project will become a huge part of your role for an extended period of time. You can expect heavy involvement from the signed LOI through Day 1 and beyond, depending on your role related to adoption (which we will discuss in Chapter 6).

If you are at a larger firm with teams that handle technology, compliance, legal, and finance, you will have to inform the key individuals from those areas about how the other firm operates. The integration team will be eager to know the answers to all the questions you've been asking in light of their specific areas of expertise.

Tech Tip 1: Make sure to obtain technology contracts and agreements (existing or pending) for:

- Software Licenses
- Maintenance and Support for hardware or software
- Any other technology services

You should also confirm if there are confidentiality and nondisclosure agreements in place with any vendors that have access to your firm's data or your clients' data.

At smaller firms, you may not have these segmented departments. Either you will handle the management of these areas or you'll split the responsibilities of integration across your implementation team. For example, someone will need to review the contracts mentioned in the above Tech Tip. This job is best delegated to someone from IT, compliance, legal or finance. It's an area of interest to each group and your responsibility is to ensure the job will get done by the most relevant and responsible party.

Tech Tip 2: For those who handle finance and IT, they will want to see IT budgets and actual financials from the prior few years as well as answers to the following questions:

- How much has been a "buy and try" approach versus a consistent investment, following a formal IT plan with a budget in sync?
- Were consultants used and if so, why?
- Were there issues that couldn't be resolved internally or was outside help part of the growth plan?

These answers will help shape the picture of how important technology has been and hopefully how well it has been managed.

Start to Meet Internally

This is the time to start regular weekly internal meetings with your implementation team. Depending on the size of the firm and what roles each individual has, the leader of this team will often be the key operations manager, director, or even the COO. Some larger firms have carved out specific roles to focus on business development and often this role takes charge of the implementation team.

During each meeting you'll want a standing agenda to cover:

- Legal agreement updates—a status of where things stand with the deal itself.
- Upcoming objectives—what is the priority of big picture items that need to be accomplished?
- Takeaways—what key items need to happen in the following days and weeks from each department?

The team lead will organize both the internal meetings as well as arrange the meetings for all involved parties at both firms when that time comes. They will arrange for data and document sharing, possibly through a shared cloud application as discussed previously. The team lead is like an air traffic controller for this integration process. They won't be doing everything, but they are the one who is responsible for making sure everything which needs to get done, is actually getting done.

Systems Integration

While some firms have separate IT departments and others have an IT person or team, each will need to know the systems, the data, what information goes where, and when it needs to get there in order to move forward with the integration process.

As you meet with the other firm's operations people, you'll want to know specifics around:

- Where is their data stored?
- How will you obtain access to this data?
- When will it be appropriate to share access to this data?
- Will it be formatted correctly for migration?
- What type of cleanup, if any, do we anticipate?

Start with Your Vendors and Custodians

In addition to your internal integration team, you're going to work heavily with your vendors and custodians at this point. Whether it's with an existing relationship for your firm, with software you plan to keep, or a new relationship that is starting because of the merger or acquisition, you will rely heavily on key vendors for the migration of data onto one platform.

As we've already mentioned, vendors for all your critical systems should be notified as soon as both parties are comfortable sharing that you are working on a potential deal. You don't need to give names and you may not even know specifics about the other firm's data initially. But once you are heavy into due diligence, it will be important to get into more details with your vendors.

The custodians will also be highly involved for the migration of financial accounts held at the other firm. Although not a system you have to migrate, from a tech and ops perspective, handling the data of investment accounts is as important as any other data belonging to your clients. The team lead or designated party will work with the custodian's relationship manager, service team, and usually a department of the custodian that specializes in M&A transitions.

Together they will handle the movement of assets whether already held with your same custodian(s) or if transferring from another custodian. Be prepared for a significant amount of effort if assets will be moving from one custodian to another. Even if assets are not transferring and you're working within one custodian, it doesn't guarantee there will be little to no work involved. The amount of effort will depend on how the joining firm's client agreements have been written. Between your compliance team and the custodian's legal team, they will verify what needs to be done to transition the accounts from the name of one RIA to another.

Survey of All Systems

From your inventory, there are a number of systems to attend to for integration. You'll want to prioritize the plan for each system, so let's take a look at what you need to address.

Necessary Hardware

Necessities to be up and running as a business on Day 1 include:

- Network connections
- Servers
- Routers
- Phone systems
- Security

The amount of work involved here will be dependent on whether or not you are in different locations. If the new firm is at an additional location, there will be a more complex workload to figure out details with the internet, phone, and cable providers, in addition to the server's location.

A different office also requires good technical equipment for communication. For quality conference and video calls, you'll need to invest in microphones, speakers, cameras, TVs, and/or projectors that will position you for handling your regular long-distance and regular communications. These items may not be your top priority for Day 1, but they will help the ongoing relationship between locations.

Other items which are commonly overlooked when addressing hardware are security systems and cameras. How you keep the doors locked and what you will use for surveillance monitoring should be addressed as a component of necessary hardware.

Desktops, laptops, printers, scanners, and mobile devices are also necessary hardware components. You'll need to decide with the onboarding group if they plan to standardize all of this equipment with your preferred providers or if you will keep what they have until their contracts run out and consider changes then. The benefit of being on standard devices is that your IT people will have the optimal amount of control across the company. They will be well positioned for maintaining standards of consistent usage, support and upgrades with a known quantity of vendors, including any maintenance with third-party providers.

Whether you have an outsourced IT provider, an in-house specialist, or if the IT person is you—hardware is a critical component to address as part of your Day 1 plan. That being said, do not give these decisions undo time or attention. Don't make it more complicated than necessary but remember to put these decisions into your plan early on.

Critical Systems

Critical Systems to be integrated with data migration (to do the work clients hire you to do) include the:

- CRM system
- Portfolio management system
- Trading and rebalancing software
- Financial planning software

When we start to talk about software that each firm uses, it's important not only to know what system is used, but how it is being used. You'll need to know if the software has been customized or if it is used out-of-the-box. In addition, ask about what is being done within the software versus what has been built manually or exported to another program for manipulation, like Excel. If you and the other company have the same core systems, do not assume that you use them in the same way or that your combined data will fit perfectly into the final agreed upon format. A good deal of time and attention should be dedicated to confirming your fields, language and formatting will merge well together.

A critical consideration in these systems involves the processes each firm is employing. Depending on how the business is structured, generally you will want to standardize across the entire firm all processes which in turn are embedded in your CRM and other systems. Generally, this is why the CRM is a great place to start for your integration efforts.

Document management systems and any additional cloud storage are critical to client service and support. So whether you use a simple network folder structure or an outside software system, you will need to decide on a consistent framework for where files will live in the future (or, at a minimum, where they will live at Day 1).

Also, do not forget to consider basic productivity software for email, documents, spreadsheets, and the like as a critical system. It may seem trivial since there are only a couple of primary systems used (Microsoft Office and Google Suite), but this will be a vital component of Day 1 productivity for the whole team. Be sure your IT team is wrapped in early on the plan for this system.

Other Important Software

We recommend moving the following important software onto one system, even though little to no data migration is required:

- Billing, accounting, and expense management software
- Forms management software
- Digital signature tools
- Compliance/cybersecurity software
- Email encryption
- Client vault or portal
- Aggregation software

- Digital planning or investment solutions
- Instant messaging
- Virtual private network access
- Learning management system

You may consider many of these systems to be vital for Day 1 of your integration, so it's important to talk through which systems will be used at that point and what changes may need to be made before then. Keeping your implementation team up to speed with these decisions will help them as they plan out their areas as well.

Ancillary Software

We suggest narrowing down the following ancillary software:

- Research and analytics software
- Risk analysis software
- Web conferencing tools
- Automated calendaring
- Conference call provider
- Dictation service

There are cases where utilizing more than one system serves a purpose for the combined use and benefit by all. And some of these systems may not even be a part of your firm today, but I would suggest being open to what the new firm is bringing to the table and be willing to make changes. Although final decisions may not happen for the official hard close and announcement to clients, you should plan to address these systems during your first year together and then come up with a time frame for broader usage or a deadline to phase them out.

The Company Website

We consider the company website to be a collaborative responsibility where both the marketing and technology members of the implementation team will need to work together. Most websites have links to an online portal, a client vault, and a custodian's online client access. Although marketing will guide the layout of the website, each of these links is managed in conjunction with your firm's technology and will need IT's support.

How Do You Decide What System to Use and When to Begin Using It?

Often, the discussions on which software or systems to utilize will take place during the due diligence phase. If these conversations do not happen naturally, you'll want to add these integration decisions to the agenda for the team's regular meetings.

In terms of choosing which software to use, the most important decision factor is to pick the best solution for your identifiable desired outcomes as a combined entity. And more importantly, considerations on where the firm is going (VISION) should drive decisions about technology. Obviously, both firms existed using their software before the deal and inevitably, there were pros and cons to each system. But in the end, your decision makers need to be both comfortable with and confident in the systems which will allow the firm to carry out the stated objectives for clients, advisors, and staff.

> In many M&As, one firm becomes the dominant entity. In an acquisition, it can be a clear-cut decision to go with the acquiring firm's established software and systems—but it shouldn't be a given. In a merger, there may be more options to discuss, but it could be a similar situation as in an acquisition, with one firm heavily influencing decisions. Either way, software choices require discussion and should not be made unilaterally.

Functionality, Support, Maintenance, and Cost

By this point in your due diligence, you should understand both firms' systems well enough to lay them side by side and be able to compare what is gained or lost by going from one system to another. You should be able to tell what the actual functionality provided by each looks like. You should also understand the support needs, maintenance, and costs involved for each. If you don't have a handle on these aspects of their systems, you'll need to spend more time asking about usage and understanding each system's benefits.

For example, some CRM systems may have different integrations which will make one system much more valuable than another in relation to your firm's long-term goals. Combine your knowledge of the potential CRM's functionality and capabilities with the firm's desired outcomes to make the best decision with which CRM you should use moving forward.

You also need to consider what kind of support and maintenance will be required and available in the future. Is the migration from one system to another going to be a capacity problem? Will you have the staff to support the maintenance of each system? Do the current vendors used by each firm provide services acceptable for the combined entity's size and scale? Never minimize the important role of who in your firm will be responsible for managing all of your various systems and what this support will look like well into the future.

Cost is also a factor to weigh in your decision on which systems to employ. Vendors are happy to help, but the migration work doesn't usually come free. Ask your vendors for help and ask what that help will cost. Now think beyond hard dollars and cents—expand to the time requirements of your staff and support services. Consider the complexity of the system and how much time your team will need to get up to speed. How steep will the learning curve be? How difficult and time-consuming will the migration of data for each system be? The hidden costs can add up quickly, so it's important to consider them in your decision making process. However, be very careful not to "save" money by NOT utilizing the right help. Vendors and consultants can provide technical expertise that may save hundreds of hours of staff time worth many times more than the cost.

Do We Want One System ASAP?

When considering whether or not to push for having one particular system by Day 1 and wondering if that's even possible or best given your time frame, you may ask if one system is even necessary. My answer is what one of my favorite college professors used to say about many situations in the business world: "It depends."

If you're aware that going to one system makes sense for the future of your company and it aligns with the direction of the firm, then getting there sooner rather than later is recommended.

Running dual systems side by side is decidedly inefficient. It's both costly and time-consuming. It can also keep your team split and detract from the cultural integration you want to see happen for this new entity. Keeping two systems also forces you to pay for support, both internal and possibly external, to keep both systems functioning well.

On the other hand, if you work through your plan and still aren't sure of what system will be the firm's long-term winner, it's not worth rushing into a decision simply to have the decision made. You want to take enough time to evaluate the options with how well they align with both the needs and the firm's goals in the future.

While preparing for a change in systems, consider potential disruptions to a number of areas with ongoing processes. There is the existing customer servicing as well as managing open task requests and executing on trades. You'll also need to think about the current workflows and any future reminders already in the system. Lastly, evaluate the effect a change will have on upcoming marketing events and regular client communications. Thinking through each of these disruptions may help you decide on the timing of your system changes.

Executing the Integration Plan

Think back to when you first started with your current vendor. What did they do to get you on board? To execute on your migrations, have a plan with the vendor of each system. Adding a new team's data is going to be a similar process to your own onboarding. Each vendor will be your go-to for how to merge two systems together.

There are two primary focal points for your integration plan: Day 1 Functionality and Data Capture.

Day 1 functionality: You will need a full list of expectations for which systems, resources, and data are necessary for Day 1 functionality. Look at your necessary hardware and critical systems list first. These are your top priorities.

Data capture: Those who control that systems' data today, whether outside vendors or internal technical folks, will be the ones to work on the actual data mapping and migration from one system to another. Each system to merge or migrate has data that ultimately needs to be housed in one spot. One firm told me that what they requested from their new counterpart was, "We'll take as much data as you can give us."

Triage

My aunt was a pediatric emergency room nurse for almost 30 years and one of the key parts of her job was triage. Triage is the idea of treating each patient in the order of the urgency of their need. If you've ever taken a sick child to an emergency room, you've probably seen triage in action: the child who is having trouble breathing after an allergic reaction takes priority over the one who swallowed a paperclip but is playing quietly in the waiting room. Triage is making assessments and then treating the most critical first.

This is the same thing that you will be doing with systems. What you work on first depends on what's most critical for your Day 1 needs. As in the medical field and as we discussed previously, timing matters. One of the best ways I've found to narrow down what will take priority is to ask myself or my team *What can wait?*

If you have limited time, say three months or less, then identify the very minimum requirements you have for Day 1. From there, focus on those major systems to support what your team has decided are essential for launch.

If you have time to work with all the vendors of the critical systems prior to launch, consider yourself fortunate. But many of us have a short time frame with varying levels of complexity of current usage. So it might not be possible to deal with all the vendors in a short period of time, say within three to six months.

It would be my least desired (worst case) scenario to start on Day 1 with the absolute minimums in place. Day 1 minimum requirements would be: the deal being inked and the clients being able to authorize accounts to be moved under one single RIA, but nothing more. My preference is to have the absolute minimums, many of the critical systems, and a plan or process in place for everything else.

At the top of my priority list are the necessary hardware decisions, followed by the critical software systems to be migrated together. Beyond that, have an updated plan for billing, which is good to have in place prior to Day 1. But again, this could be done without changing systems or migrating any data. Each firm has had a system in place up to this point and you can continue to use what you have, if necessary. You just need to decide what you want to be done, in light of what is feasible and move forward accordingly.

Start with the very minimum. From there, it's all about prioritizing which systems are most important to you and your firm and how you plan to operate given your time frame.

Current Projects

Something else to consider during implementation is to identify what projects are already in progress at each firm. You want to know what costs have been incurred thus far and what the costs will be for completing these projects as scheduled. Once you get this information, you'll have decisions to make as to what should continue and what needs to be cut.

One firm I spoke to told me about their existing work toward considering a change of their portfolio management system when they were considering an acquisition. Instead of abandoning this project to switch systems, they realized their targeted software was what the other firm was already using. So, instead of rushing to integrate two systems, they let both systems continue when the deal closed. Essentially this became an in-house extended demo for the primary firm and by six months in, they were nearing a decision on which system to use.

Custodial Involvement

Custodial involvement isn't usually considered part of tech directly, but the custodian's data is extremely relevant at this stage and definitely a high priority when bringing two firms together. If you're transferring accounts, your custodian may provide a template for migrating accounts or specific directions on how their paperwork needs to be filled out.

Your plan for integrating here must include how much time will be spent on preparing the new firm's data for a clean transfer. Often, this means data cleanup will be necessary and this means more time by either you or others from the joining firm. Again, this is a big role for the main operations leader on the implementation team.

Handling the account changes paperless is also a consideration. These days, many firms would like to look for a paperless transaction with their custodians, but you need to understand what that means for the whole project. Consider if the client base is used to paperless technology. Is your staff accustomed to paperless technology? And you'll need to know if your custodians offer paperless technology options for every type of account or activity related to the accounts in question.

Coordinating a Comprehensive Implementation Plan

One firm explained how important it was to gain strong buy-in up from the top executives at both firms, as well as the managers and the staff. The operations team built out a written plan, including details such as what technology might be staying and what may go away, and shared the high-level objectives across the firm. They wanted everyone to know the combined firm's direction. The plan included a clear explanation of those responsible for making decisions at each level, which is a crucial component for a successful transition.

Their plan was to segregate the different components of the firm, so they would not be stuck having one person or group trying to tackle so many (too many) pieces all at once. The integration was split by the areas of their investment workstream, technology used, operations workflows, compliance needs, legal agreements, and marketing activities.

This is an excellent example of the major players having a comprehensive plan to bring multiple departments of a firm together in a coordinated fashion.

In order to complete your integration plan, ensuring a smooth transfer of the client's investment accounts, seek to know as much as you can about the firm joining you, their clients, and the abilities of your combined integration team.

Next, we're going to explore the necessity of integrating system usage through policies and procedures.

Policy and Procedure Integration

Closely related to the integration of technology is the integration of policies and procedures, or how things get done within a firm. It's vital to start the merge process by addressing what the future state of each firm's processes and procedures will be. If your new counterpart firm has a policies and procedures manual and you haven't seen it yet, ask for it now. A compliance manual will be a suitable alternative, as it usually offers a good amount of policy and procedure information.

One important question you want to ask here is: Will accommodations stay as they are today? Things like fee exceptions, report customizations, and certain client communications might all have to be talked through. You want to know what the combined entity is going to be okay with going forward. You will need to know who is in charge of decision making at this level before moving forward. Establishing that early on will play an important role in the ease of answering these questions.

For most firms, policies and procedures related to technology will come in the form of checklists and documented outlines of their standard procedures. You will want your key people in each functional area to review the current procedures of your new counterpart firm. Then, an assessment will be needed to determine how close their procedures line up with your firm's way of doing things.

Tech decisions are difficult because it always takes longer than you think it would. There are always little issues that come up due to differences in how each firm operates. It can be easier to merge procedures if you have the same tech, but even then, it's not a given that everything will line up perfectly.

Open Communication About Upcoming Changes

Many firms will find benefits from coming together, strengthening each other in ways where separately they had been weak. One firm I spoke to shared how they felt like they had some compliance gaps prior to their merger. They were very excited about combining firms which would quickly bridge the gap and lead to noticeable improvements in compliance almost immediately. This helps not only the individuals involved at the firm, but the combined firm as a whole, as well as the clients they serve.

But not everyone is as open to change. Beyond the technology changes, your team will also be thinking about what else will be different. Some will realize that procedural changes will impact roles within the firm. Those who executed trades, prepared client reports, handled marketing mailings, and did compliance reviews previously may not be the same people doing those jobs within the new entity.

Some people may ask questions and verbalize their concerns, but there will also be some who won't ask these questions openly. It's important to communicate as much as you can about what will be changing and how you will lead them through it.

A Real-Life Example of Policy and Procedures Integration Challenges

The firms in HIFON are all different sizes and shapes. One firm I spoke to had about 50 employees and were acquiring a practice which would bring in an additional 4 employees. Initially, the thought from the ops side was that they were starting small, so this transition and integration should be simple. Yet as the small firm joined the larger entity, it became clear that not enough was done up front to communicate policy and procedure expectations.

In the first six months after the acquisition, the adjustments the larger firm expected of the smaller firm were simply not happening. And the perception was that it felt like this smaller group was essentially renting space and not operating as one unified group. It was as if they got married as a formality but continued to live two separate lives.

For example, client service was handled in two entirely different ways between the smaller and larger groups. The larger firm had a segmented approach to who and how clients were met with, while the smaller team met with all clients quarterly and ran full financial plan updates regularly, without exception.

The lessons learned were twofold:

- Never underestimate the importance of setting detailed front-end expectations about how you expect your new teammates to operate and how that integrates with the flow of your firm's operations.
- Understand that the process of change for a new group takes time. It isn't simply hearing information and applying it immediately. This process isn't quick and won't happen overnight.

The ops leaders realized they were not as detailed in their policy and procedures communications at the beginning of the process prior to the deal being done and that they should have made more of an effort early on, no matter the size of the firm merging in.

Culture Integration

Why are we talking about culture in a chapter on tech implementation? Well, because the successful steps of integration start with the systems, lead to the procedures, and are topped off with culture.

Because you want to inspire your teams to work well together and galvanize the start of this deal, you need to invest heavily in getting the tech platform right. This goal is important because the tech is what everyone will use every day to do their job well. So don't miss your opportunity to provide for your staff in this way. Tech glitches can be costly not only in productivity and morale, but ultimately to the impact on clients.

How your firm's culture uses and thinks about technology matters in bringing together a successful M&A transaction.

Connect on a Personal Level First

Life is all about personal relationships and blending people with their technology is no different.

Admittedly it's very tempting to jump right into work (Let's not waste time!). But don't make the mistake of looking past people in order to get more work done faster. And don't think that engaging with people is simply a means to an end of increasing their productivity or buy-in. Connection with others is ultimately rewarding personally and will be advantageous to the firm and clients.

I encourage you to talk with your counterparts and take time to connect with your new members. You have similar backgrounds in ops, compliance, and technology; you have similar responsibilities and you both take a disciplined approach to your craft. This is a starting point for engagement with each other. You can build together from there.

From the Start, Spend Time Together

As an operations leader, you want to see the technology used in-person. So arrange to sit down in a conference room and ask your new colleagues to show it to you. Do this to get a vibe for how the office hums using technology.

Spend time working in each other's offices. Do regular calls (video, if possible) for the integration team members who will have regular interaction with each other. If you are at a distance, invest in travel—both ways. Spend the time and the money to make these things happen. Connecting key people early is important; don't overlook its benefits.

Once you are familiar with the daily usage, you'll be in a position to verify if the two firms are speaking the same language. You will figure this out by comparing actions, running them side by side, and by showing each other. Verify the procedure with multiple team members if possible, not just those in charge.

Similar to systems and procedures, there is no easy answer if you find out there are differences in your procedural language. In the end, be cognizant of "us" versus "them" language and stick to identifying the best outcome for the new firm, as a whole.

A Real-Life Example of Cultural Integration Challenges

One of the firms I spoke to felt culture fit might be a big obstacle to overcome during their acquisition. In this case, a larger firm was acquiring a smaller team who was going to see a great change by doing things a new way. There was confidence they would integrate smoothly.

But things didn't go the way they expected.

It didn't take much time for the tension to get thick. The acquiring firm found themselves dealing with an ops individual with a very protective personality who was not very open to a new way of doing things, nor interested in the core firm's ways. Instead of being open to change and willing to be objective, the flow of work stayed personal, the same, and void of what the acquiring firm thought were centralized team benefits for all parties involved, given the larger firm's size and scale.

The acquiring firm started to share their expectations with the ops individual in smaller bite-sized pieces, hoping to ease the challenge of this transition. Given time, space, and improved communications, the new firm acclimated.

Looking back, the acquiring firm would have spent more time up front communicating what integrating their systems, procedures, and culture meant for the smaller firm; that integration was necessary from Day 1 and that change was required from both sides—neither would continue to do what they'd always done as separate entities.

Also, the ops leaders of the acquiring firm would have spent a little less time with the higher-ups of the new firm, and more time with the people that actually do the ops work. Without an established connection to the employees, the acquiring ops leaders felt like they were walking on eggshells around their new team.

We all learn from our mistakes and this firm now knows that combining cultures should be detailed (even documented) early on as part of the integration process. They now use a list to communicate culture expectations and they no longer assume the new team will know how to get things done their way. Also, they no longer accept the phrase "we do it the same way" without seeing proof first. If this integration could be done all over again, the larger firm would have explicitly expressed the necessity for all team members to be additive to the culture from Day 1, rather than detractive.

Takeaways from This Example

Although you'll get the 30,000-foot view from the higher-ups, it's incredibly important to hear from all employees. Listening to those who are both doing the work and interacting as a new member of an established team will give you valuable perspective about their feelings and perceptions.

Empathize with the fact that it's intimidating for a new person to come into an existing team to do similar (if not the same) work but with different procedures. He or she may not even know everyone's names on this new larger team. Help your existing team by having a plan in place for integrating new team members. Clear direction will help the rest of the team feel like they're doing the right thing even if there is some tension early on. Allow your teammates to talk out their feelings and perceptions. Once you know what they are thinking, it can be a totally different ball game and lead to important breakthroughs for integration.

Wild Cards

What If You Can't Come to an Agreement on a Particular System or Procedure?

First off, this is normal. In fact, I might worry if both sides completely agree to everything the other wants or asks for, without any pushback. Ownership and protectiveness is to be expected, if not a sign of a healthy working relationship with your firm's systems and technology. It's okay to take your time when agreements can't be made, but also recognize if your "we'll decide this later" category starts to get full. You *will* need to start making some of these decisions soon.

If trade-offs are needed, it's reasonable to compromise with something you don't consider a big deal. But when we're talking about the critical systems and the very important software needing data integration, stick close to your objectives and your line of authority for decision making. Let policies and procedures be the pieces to adjust as the group works together toward a solution.

What If You Get More Time with the New Advisors (the "Higher-Ups") Than the New Operations and Technology People?

This is another common situation, especially when smaller groups join into a larger firm. You might get the primary advisor's time and attention even though he or she may or may not really know the ins and outs of the technology or the ops side of procedures.

In this scenario, I would recommend two things:

1. Try to work time in with the ops people, even if it's just a few general conversations. Anything you can do to directly spend time with them will help you to better understand their world.
2. Sometimes #1 isn't an option ("they're just too busy to meet") so if there is an advisor at the new firm giving you their attention, take it and gather as much information about their team's tech systems and usage as you can. Ask questions. Dig into the details. If any of their answers lack depth, it's a signal to find out more. Their answers may lead you to where you need to go next for the details you want.

What If You Don't Have Specialized Tech Point-Person?

Amy Flourry, Director of Operations at Rehmann Financial in Lansing, MI, says that having someone who knows and understands how to move and map data correctly, on both sides of the deal, is a critical piece in an M&A transaction. "Whether you're using the data to populate custodial paperwork, to communicate with clients, or to manage your practice and the progress of your merger, it is critical you get the right people involved. You don't need people who are employed in a technical role, but you do need people who know and understand what the data means and how to properly use the data to accomplish your objectives," she says.

Flourry shared how it's possible for each individual at a firm to use technology in a slightly different way, so it can be a problem if you, as the ops leader, don't factor in the various perspectives and uses as you integrate.

She added, "Your own paperwork may be filled out using the new or existing firm's technology. At a minimum, it's imperative that you can trust in the integrity and accuracy of the data, that you understand how to properly use it, and finally, that you store the historical and updated data so that it is easily accessible as you move forward."

Ongoing Projects or Everything Else Already in Motion

Every day, your time and attention is already dedicated to client service, advisor support, ongoing projects, seasonal activities, and new firm initiatives. Being fully committed with your current workload makes it harder to dedicate time to an M&A integration project.

One firm told me about the challenges they faced when an acquisition took place in the middle of a significant structural change. They were moving from silo practices to a true ensemble structure—a sizable shift for any firm—when the ops team learned that the owners had intentions to merge in another firm. So while they transitioned internally, a process involving plenty of change and time investment by the operations and client service teams, it was necessary for their focus to be shared between the current initiative and this upcoming merger. It wasn't impossible to handle both, but it certainly changed how they lead their team through the structural change. The timing quickly put their updated practices to the test and it left little time for hand holding internally.

Be sure that those in your firm who are driving toward any M&A activity are aware of your firm's current major projects and ongoing initiatives. Keep in mind, this information probably won't slow down a deal, but hopefully the decision makers will consider the big picture of capacity needs when they discuss the deal's timing.

Time for a Tech Cleanup?

Consider what technology is rarely used and ask if it should be eliminated. Question the frequency of usage of systems to identify potential waste. Is an entire system sitting idle? Are checklists once thought to be crucial now collecting electronic dust? It's a satisfying accomplishment to finally get rid of technology that's been hanging around for too long.

As we've said before, be sensitive to existing usage. You don't want to remove technology that fills a role for some group or team. But don't be afraid to assess the costs (time, support, and money) involved in the use and maintenance of a system against the benefits of its termination.

Other Matters to Consider

The whole integration stage differs depending on many of the following factors:

People and vendors: This process will appear different depending on how many people are involved and how many vendors you are dealing with. Integration will change based on if you will be dealing with multiple vendors or with just one vendor. Roles and personalities of those involved will also play a part in what integration looks like.

The terms of the agreement: Is this an acquisition where one firm is clearly taking the lead? Or is it a true merger of two equals where both parties have equal say? Your transition process will look different based on how and why the deal was created.

Vantage point: Where .are people coming from and what does their future look like? Some deals happen because a company is looking for a life raft to save a failing enterprise. Some companies are in decent shape but are looking for increased scale to put themselves in a much better position. And some are fully confident where they are, but the M&A activity is driven by a succession plan for aging owners.

With more people, the viewpoints and opinions can spread out like shotgun spray. As the ops leader, you're the one responsible to bring all these thoughts and ideas under control. This process can be complex, especially given the constraints on your time and resources.

There is one constant, though, no matter what size and shape of a company you are working with—you still have to teach new people to learn new systems and get them to use new processes. So the more help you have within your whole integration team, the easier this endeavor will be to accomplish.

Real-Life Examples

Baggage: In speaking with a number of firms about their experiences, many used the term "baggage" when talking about what certain groups bring with them to the new entity. From culture, personalities, or whatever it may be, every group carries around items they don't want to let go. Depending on that firm's culture, introducing different procedures can feel like you're trying to steal their suitcase, discard or rearrange everything they had inside, and stuff it full of your own belongings—instead of leaving the things that were working well for them up until that point alone.

<u>Slowing down data transfer:</u> Another firm's experience was making the decision to pull in data based on what was available for migration before the close date. Since the team they were acquiring was not fully in control of the technology where they came from, the approach was driven by what data they had. They started with a data dump from the prior CRM system into their existing system. Unfortunately for their portfolio management, they were not able to bring anything with them so they had to start fresh as assets transferred in.

Although they had access to their prior database of planning related data, their need for this information was not immediate for each client relationship. The thought was if it's not used in the first year when connecting with the client, it may not be needed. It turned out to be less of a migration and instead a 12-month rolling transition of relevant data, which spread out the work and put less pressure on the integration team leading up to their Day 1.

<u>Data doesn't always line up:</u> One firm found themselves in a situation where they had the benefit of being on some similar systems with the firm they were looking to acquire.

They were on the same document management system, which ended up being a painless transition. Both firms shared the same financial planning software as well. Unfortunately, their two big systems (CRM and Portfolio Management) were different. So for the CRM migration, they hired a consultant who helped them map the data. But for some of the data, it was like a square peg going into a round hole. It's just wasn't lining up and would require a lot of cleanup.

For the data extraction from the portfolio management system, they took in 15 years of data on 700 accounts. This turned out to be a big challenge primarily due to a lack of full participation from the new firm's team (a Wild Card noted in Chapter 4), and they needed help answering questions. In the end, the vendor importing the data helped, although they did end up with some performance issues after the data load (due to things like pricing files missing for bonds). Teasing out all of this took time before they got it right.

We intentionally left out vendor names in our real-life examples because we don't want to make claims about which vendors can or cannot do certain actions. We recommend that you consult directly with your vendors to see how they can help you with your M&A integration activities. With the potential of stating the obvious, most of your vendors will be happy to help you work through the process of bringing more business their way.

Key Takeaways

The implementation stage is the culmination of your team's hard work during the strategy, due diligence, and assessment phases. Understanding that there will be unique challenges to navigate—implementing new systems and processes while also simultaneously merging cultures, building relationships and balancing the ongoing needs of the business—is key to a successful transition. To help mitigate these challenges:

- Get the right people involved on your integration team early
- Have a strong due diligence process
- Build a plan for prioritizing systems integration based on firm objectives and your future state of technology
- Seek help from your vendors for data integration
- Establish early your decision makers on policy and procedures going forward
- Understand that cultural integration is part of a successful merging of technology, data, and usage

Implementation is a busy phase. The music seems to start playing all at once, and in addition to technology the firm is likely dealing with updating forms for compliance and custodian transfers, reviewing potential changes to advisory agreements, addressing billing changes, and digging in to update marketing materials. Amidst all the distractions and important projects vying for your attention, it's key to prioritize, or triage, so the top systems are ready for your needs when you decide to launch.

Greg's Final Word

It may be tempting during this phase of the integration for leadership to disengage while the project managers, leads and operations teams kick off the implementation process. While it may feel like your "heavy lifting" is done, your role is no less important, it just transitions from leading to supporting.

Your goal is to listen, calm anxiety, put out fires, and offer resources to remove any obstacles that may pop up along the way. In addition, you need to repeat—and repeat—your vision of success and why the efforts being undertaken are very important. In particular you also need to clearly articulate "WIIFM"—the "what's in it for me" for each and every employee in successfully completing the integration work. Your communication and your attitude can also deeply impact the success of this stage. Are you enthusiastic about the next phase of your firm? Are you offering positive feedback for those in the trenches? These seemingly small things matter, especially when they come from you.

Yes, there will be speed bumps, which you should expect, and oftentimes they deal with scope and timelines. This integration certainly isn't the only thing happening at your firm, and timelines get pushed back. Resources get thin. Scope creeps as you learn more about what your technology can and can't do.

Problem-solving becomes a major part of your role in this stage, and people will depend on you to make informed but swift decisions. Be ready to build some flexibility into your timelines. Adjust when needed but continue moving forward. Keep tabs on stress factors and the bandwidth of your team. Stay close to team leads, operations, and project managers. Encourage open communication. Your continuous and positive support of these efforts is critical for success!

6

Rollout and Adoption

Technology may be an essential part of our business, but it is only truly effective if it is accepted and used consistently and systematically across the firm. Now that you've implemented the programs across firms and have integrated the technology and its workflows and processes, it's time to promote its adoption. In this phase, your goal is to solidify new thinking, help your teammates make new mental connections, and ultimately establish new habits. These habits that are built around the technology will carry your firm into the future—together, as a combined entity. In this chapter, I will share my strategy and tactics for encouraging tech adoption including communication plans, milestone setting, and incentive programs for training and ongoing education. From there Shaun will take you through his steps for ensuring that your hard-earned technology integration starts paying off dividends in efficiency and growth.

The Three E's of Leadership: Enthusiasm, Efficiency, Example

It starts—AGAIN—by rallying all the troops to begin the adoption phase. Share an overall vision, one that requires everyone's participation and benefits the entire firm. The first rule of adoption from a leadership perspective is to make sure people have a clear understanding of "why" we're doing this—and how it fits into your overall strategy and what's required to be successful.

As a leader, it's important that you exude **enthusiasm** through every step of this process. Communicate your excitement about where you're

© The Author(s) 2018
G. Friedman and S. Kapusinski, *The Financial Advisor M&A Guidebook*,
https://doi.org/10.1007/978-3-030-00003-5_6

headed and stress the importance of each team and individual in their role in achieving adoption goals. Positivity can be contagious coming from you, especially in times when confidence can be a little uncertain.

It's also important that your enthusiasm is backed up with **efficient** processes for achieving those goals—Shaun will cover much of this in the following section on the actual execution of adoption. But speaking from experience, nothing throws a wrench into forward movement and momentum like bottlenecks, confusion, and delays. Be clear about where you want to go and when, but also HOW you would like to see the team get there. Encourage consistent and repeatable processes for each segment of adoption through training. Capture these processes so that everyone has clarity about their expectations. When an unforeseen issue pops up, be available to help resolve it quickly.

Real adoption comes from seeing progress through regular checkups. It's natural to have a sense of pride when accomplishing certain milestones, and to take this a step further, consider implementing incentive programs for completing training segments—much like obtaining a license or certification—and attach them to bonus programs. It's made a big difference in how adoption is perceived in my firm as we build awareness, promote education and reward individuals for their efforts.

Lastly, lead by **example**. It's not enough to be excited about the future and to push for the team to learn new processes and use new systems. You actually have to roll up your sleeves and learn the new processes and systems yourself. That's not to say you'll be a power user by any stretch—you just need to show, not tell, that you're as all in as every member of your team.

Tech Adoption Gone Wrong

Sometimes no amount of due diligence, research, and cost analysis can prevent a technology mistake. Some years ago, not too long after Private Ocean's formation, we determined that a new document management solution was in order. It aligned with our growth strategy and there were new options on the market at the time that seemed to fit our changing needs.

So we went through a long process and chose a new technology solution, feeling confident in our decision. We purchased the licenses, pushed through with implementation and started the adoption phase. It was at that point—deep into the process—that I was faced with what was shaping up to be a company revolt on my hands. Multiple teams expressed their unhappiness, pushed back, and were in general very frustrated with the direction we were taking.

Why?

- We didn't perform enough due diligence, we didn't pilot the product, and we rushed through the assessment phase.

- We didn't give the existing vendor the opportunity to discuss our needs and how they could accommodate us.
- The product was not a good fit given our team's reliance on the existing platform and how they were accustomed to using it.
- The change triggered a cultural shift that was disruptive and unnecessary.

Even though these were the top two systems available, we simply moved from one to the other for the wrong reasons. In this case, I heard the team loud and clear and we abandoned the new system and reverted back to our existing one. This was a costly mistake on our part as far as license fees and time and resources spent, but one that came with many lessons to be learned. Do your homework and don't skip steps! Get more stakeholders involved and do more due diligence. Get better buy-in. The worst-case scenario in the adoption stage might seem to be one where a product is abandoned, but it's far worse when you go completely through the process of implementation and training only to have your staff actively avoid using the product and finding workarounds that lead to fragmented, inconsistent usage.

Now that you've sparked some excitement and incentivized the team to move toward an effective adoption, it's time to start preparing to learn your new systems and programs. Shaun walks us through his approach for an efficient, organized process.

Adoption Preparation

Having operational involvement in a growing advisory firm, you're quite familiar with the constant and ongoing nature of change in the workplace. You also realize the importance of organization for your firm's operations and employ strategies like checklists—for everything from onboarding new clients to running quarterly reports, in order to help your employees do what needs to be done, *especially* when there is a change in procedure.

In their 2010 book, *Switch*,[1] Chip Heath and Dan Heath wrote about the difficulties inherent to change. One takeaway from their book is how building habits lessen the impact of change. So let me ask, how strategic have you been with building new habits for yourself? How about for those on your team? Do you assist your teammates with change by offering tools, like the

---

[1]Heath, C., and Heath, D. (2010). *Switch: How to Change Things When Change Is Hard.* The Crown Publishing Group, New York.

checklists we mentioned above? Or do you make changes, tell them about it, and hope for the best?

Our goal with adoption is to help you transition your new teammates from simply knowing about the systems, procedures, and technology—to being loyal to them. This takes time, but you can make a big dent with some simple strategies.

At this point, your due diligence is complete, you've hashed out the inventory, made decisions on systems, and worked toward the big data migration and steps for implementation—all while getting to know the folks who will soon be your new teammates. It's been a lot of effort. Yet when it comes to preparing for successful adoption, it's hard to know what exactly will work best for this new group.

We've already mentioned how important it is to spend time with everyone from the incoming team as it relates to learning their existing systems, usage, and technology. And we talked in the previous chapter about learning their culture and trying to get a feel for what makes the team click (or not). It's equally important to learn what you can about each person and what makes them tick as individuals.

You want to know what they like and don't like about each of their existing systems, and what is truly important to them when it comes to their technology and processes. "What don't you want to lose?" is a great question to ask.

Establishing a Foundation of Trust

As similar as some work cultures may seem on the surface, know that there will always be differences. Each person within a culture is unique with their own personality, preferences, and quirks. So keep in mind that regardless of how much you communicate and ask questions, there will still be a learning curve when it comes to how your new teammates operate in real time with the newly combined firm. In the same manner, they will need time to get to know you better, in "real time" as well. Stay consistent. There's no easier way to lose trust than not being the person that you were before the deal closed.

In order to strengthen your relationships, establish and build up a foundation of trust. The following three action items will help accomplish this:

- Finding key allies
- Communicating consistently
- Offering quality training

Finding Key Allies

Three different pairings can be your key allies during the transition of these firms coming together.

Business Owners: Your first allies should be the business owners who form a bond while making the deal come together. From the top, they can be your largest, loudest, and most influential cheerleaders. As Greg opened the chapter, they are allies to inspire and drive everyone toward the changes to come.

M&A Deal Leaders: The M&A deal leaders (which may or may not be the same as the owners) can also be key allies. These are the people who had the primary responsibility for completing the deal. Usually, these roles are pivotal with non-organic growth strategy firms. Not only is there high motivation to be successful, but these individuals typically have dynamic personalities that help attract both firms to the idea that they will become better as a combined entity.

Main Ops Leaders: The ops leads on either side can also be key allies. These roles most likely are responsible for the deal execution when it gets down to the specifics. If this is you at your firm, find the person with the same role at the other firm and champion change together. In general, this position not only does a lot of client service and behind the scenes work, but they end up being the go-to person for questions—especially on new systems or procedures.

If the owner, deal leader, or ops lead in the firm coming in has built up strong, trusting relationships with their team over time, any one of them (if not all) can play a vital role as an ally for this transition. Namely, as they prepare their team to make this large and important move, they can transfer some of the trust their people have in them—toward you, your team, and your systems. If done correctly, your key allies will have laid the foundation for trust well before you even enter the room.

Communicating Consistently

Communications can be a major hurdle for some pairs of firms coming together.

One firm I spoke to was very large, with nearly 500 employees. A total of twelve leaders made all the decisions regarding the acquisition. Because it took time from concept to implementation, there was a lot of opportunity for communication—or, in this case, miscommunication.

What started to happen was that messages were sent about who was making decisions at almost the very same time that the decisions were actually being made. The delayed communication led to a lack of trust early on and it caused confusion for the group.

Ideally, there should have been clear communication about their hierarchy. About who is setting their priorities, who everyone is going to report to, and who else is involved in providing strategic direction. You don't want people operating in confusion, uncertainty, and even fear (ex. "Will I lose my job?").

This example reinforces the need to communicate early and often about important items like the organizational chart, highlighting the project leads, as well as the strategic and operational decision makers.

Communication By the Firm's Leaders

Initially, communications to each side of the deal will be happening by their own leaders. The messaging early on focuses on all aspects of the transition, including the big "whys."

- Why is the deal happening? (Growth, scale, opportunities, geography, succession.)
- Why will your clients benefit? (Improved capabilities, better pricing, access to and attraction of talent in the marketplace.)
- Why will the team and each individual employee benefit? (Enhanced systems and technology, additional personal responsibilities, potential new career opportunities.)

From the start, the team will ask (to themselves or outright): "What's in it for me?" This is a natural and valid question, so prepare to answer it. They will want to know if their work life will be improved or if you can make it easier to do their job. Keep these things in mind as you formulate the messages you communicate moving forward.

Communication By the Operations Lead

Usually after the soft-close signing, a decision will be made for when it makes sense to start some communications that go from you over to the new group.

As a start, send a general message reinforcing the excitement about this opportunity and the benefits of the two firms coming together. Next, share a timeline so everyone starts thinking about how and when they will need to prepare. Inevitably, it will be a season with lots of change and will probably feel a bit hectic. It's good to let people look at their calendars and see what else is on their plates (both personally and professionally) as soon as possible so they can mentally adjust for what is to come.

If you are migrating a team and their data to a number of new systems, your timeline should include the following items:

- Data cleanup: There may be data sets (small and large) that could require formatting updates prior to launch. Examples include matching portfolio management system household names to CRM household names, or requiring every contact to have an email address even if they don't currently have one (Tip: a work around is using the structure firstnamelastname@noemail.invalid as a filler).
- Testing migration: If able, it's helpful to have your vendors test migration using a sample subset of data to ensure everything is mapped over correctly. This also allows time for the firm moving data to see what their data will look like in the new systems and to validate it's showing up correctly.
- Super user training: Identify a small set of users who will get their initial training before everyone else. After training these individuals, you can determine if design or procedural changes will need to be made before full team training. Not only do these users get priority training, but they will become the go-to internal users and advocates for timely and accurate adoption practices.
- Firm-wide training: Some firms provide vendor-led training via the web, whereas others provide self-study videos to prepare new users for their systems. The most common type is in-person training sessions (More on training in the next few pages).
- Final migration and launch: Pick a date for data migration on the very first timeline you share. Of course, there may be an adjustment based on how the planning and systems implementation goes, not to mention the custodial pieces we talked about in the previous chapter. It's okay to adjust this date as time goes on, based on the firm's needs and what works best for the clients. (Think: billing cycles!) But you want these key items on everyone's mind as soon as possible.

Plan to send out a message every couple of weeks to update the team on the status of the timeline—simply to keep excitement up and communication lines open. Try to get firm-wide participation in crafting these messages, including people from HR or marketing, as an example. Even if some final decisions aren't made yet, letting everyone know what's being worked on builds trust and provides comfort by removing uncertainty.

Keep your communication fresh. Feel free to change things up and have the messages go out from different people each time. You can also post messages to your intranet or have the sender share the message in video format, simply to inject a bit more life and variety into it.

Communication Through Delegation

Since there will be a smaller team of individuals, from both sides, involved in the implementation of the transition plan, more detailed communications should go to these people more often. They can then best determine how to distribute information out to their team, department, or direct reports.

These implementation team communications, whether electronic or in-person, might include items such as:

- Regular updates on the progress along the timeline
- Reinforcing agreed upon system and/or procedural changes
- FAQs on items such as IT support and resource people, clearly communicating who the new users can ask when they encounter issues or have questions.

While you may have a mind for details and a comprehensive view of what needs to get done, be sensitive to information overload. There's only so much people can take in at one given time. Not everyone down the line needs to receive and digest a three-page email every week.

Because the implementation team leads know their own people best, trust them to effectively communicate the information you give them. They will have the pulse on when to share information via email and when to share it in-person. Encourage them to check in with their team afterward. Often, the most impactful buy-in moments happen during open and impromptu discussions when questions can be freely asked and honest answers given on the spot—even if it's an "I don't know" followed by "but I'll get back to you as soon as I find out."

Offer Quality Training

As you put together your plans for a training program, first break it into two time-based groupings: Pre-Launch and Post-Launch. Next, decide if you're going to have everyone together for all training or break into smaller groups, based on role (ex. advisors and non-advisors) for certain sessions. If it's the latter, include the whole implementation team from both sides to brainstorm the best ways to train each particular group.

Are you able to get your vendors involved? If there are expenses with the vendors who are migrating the data, you may consider asking about training for the new team as part of the services they are being paid to provide.

Does your firm employ a learning management system with videos, tutorials, and quizzes to prepare new employees for your systems and procedures? If so, utilize these scalable resources as much as possible.

The majority of firms will provide multiple onsite in-person training sessions for their new teammates both Pre- and Post-Launch.

When Does Training Actually Begin?

It may sound crazy, but when you were initially communicating about what systems you use and explaining how you use them; when you were going over procedures and detailing why they work—you were actually beginning a training program. Training starts as early as the discovery phase of your due diligence process.

By sharing that initial information, you laid the groundwork for the team's integration. While working toward coming together to operate under one umbrella, you were preparing to take the best of both worlds in order to find a better future together. So, even before you think of putting together a formal training program, consider your previous communications as a frame for the picture you are creating of this newly combined firm and its entire operations.

Training Pre-launch

Quantity

In our sample timeline, we mentioned holding Super User training sessions if the team you're merging with is large enough for this to be appropriate. Schedule Super User training about 2 to 4 weeks before the general training to allow time for adjustments based on any of their feedback. As a bare minimum, consider your last few implementation team meetings as de facto training sessions. You want to be sure everyone is on the same page going into your main general training sessions.

Ideally, you want to schedule 3 to 4 in-person training sessions before your launch date for everyone from the new firm to attend.

Length

Although some team members would love their training in thirty-minute sessions, that's not enough time to get through much content. At sixty minutes, you're getting in a solid amount of information, but in my experience, it still isn't enough time. Yet, any type of meeting that lasts longer than two hours, especially if the material isn't that exciting, can be an arduous process.

At that point, typically there is less interaction from the group, and it can also end up being a waste of the additional time since retention quantity is usually low by then.

Ninety minutes is probably the longest your sessions should go before people start nodding off and checking email (or texting each other about what's for lunch).

Content

The priority of the systems you chose to move data from, or change altogether, will determine what you cover in training. For systems that are not changing (or not changing any time soon), give expectations for how long that system will be operating and maintained in its current form.

For systems changing where data is migrating, remind your new team to continue to use those systems up until the migration so good data can be moved. Some people may think it's okay not to use those systems since they're going away or changing, but you want your people to create habits which support the desired direction, so emphasize your expectation for compliance.

Content Timing

First session: Your first session's content will include a general explanation of the firm's systems, what's available, and what's going to be new or different on their Day 1. Communicate that the main focus of this training is to enable everyone to be productive right out of the gate.

You want the group to know that you understand their world and what's important to both them and their clients. Remember that this may be your first interaction with some people from the incoming group. This day will be the starting point for building your foundation of trust with every word you say, every cultural hint you give, and every joke you make. Choose your words wisely!

Second session: While your first training will focus on systems and productivity, your second session should focus on procedures.

Go through a "day in the life" for each role or department. Walk through their daily activities. Give some examples of actions you are familiar with. This is a great opportunity to ask for their input so you can describe the similarities and differences between how things currently happen and what it will look like at launch.

Third and fourth sessions can include: Department-specific breakouts—getting into systems that might only be used by certain groups of the team (ex. Custodial details for the client service team, or financial planning system material for those involved in that arena). Include a final run-through of major systems, including a short review from the first session, and a reminder of what is the same and what will be different on Day 1.

You may be quite close to launching your technology at this point and if there is some data you originally thought to move over that may not make it on Day 1, now is a good time to let everyone know what will be missing and what the plan for that data will be going forward.

Who Leads Training?

Depending on the content of the training, these sessions should be led by a combination of key people on your implementation team from both sides. From the firm coming in, there is usually one main person who is responsible for systems and technology usage. They should be involved in every session and ideally they would also cover some of the training material. At a minimum, have these individuals explain the differences between the "old way" and the "new way." Encourage them to explain how decisions were made for the items that will be changing. It will help their team with adoption if they hear both what is new, and why, from a trusted person coming from their side of the table.

From the larger or established firm handling this merger, there is also likely to be a primary person or small team responsible for systems usage. These are the most obvious choices to lead most of your training sessions. In instances where there will be more specific session or department specific information to cover the usage of their systems (such as trading procedures, custodial sites, or your company's intranet), this is a good time to bring in the SMEs from across your organization.

Who Attends?

Because you need full company buy-in and support, it's important that everyone attend the training sessions. When I say everyone, I mean everyone from the receptionist to the CEO. At a bare minimum, every advisor should attend the first and the final general sessions. If you are providing online content and educational training, have a list of nonnegotiable standards of basic training that everyone will need to complete. When identifying your standards, keep in mind that many individuals do only the minimum requirements due to capacity restraints. Don't expect everyone to go above and beyond. Assign or require training for anything you will hold them accountable for in the future.

For your "day in the life" and the department specific training sessions, split these sessions up into specific user groups. Obviously, this will depend on the size of the teams and who is actually involved in handling which functional roles. Tailor the training to your needs and what makes the most sense for your team.

Adoption 101

<u>Be Supportive</u>
Once you hit Day 1, first and foremost: be present with your new team. If they are in another office location, make sure you put your top systems and technology people onsite to reinforce usage and deal with any questions or problems that arise. Often, those first few days are hectic and potentially overwhelming (depending on how much change is happening). You want them to feel highly supported.

The process reminds me of having a baby. No matter how much you and your significant other prepare, plan, and purchase—those first few days with a newborn are the beginning of an entirely new chapter. You and your "team" are used to being in control, having a routine, knowing what comes next. (Regardless of how much training you've done.) But those first few days are uncharted territory. It's busy, unpredictable, and can feel like it's more than you can handle given everything else you do during a normal day.

In the same way, imagine advisors trying to coordinate client meetings to go over their changes and the support members working to figure out where information is stored, all while trying to get their typical daily work done. It's a lot to handle.

In their book, *In Search of Excellence,*[2] Robert Waterman, Jr. and Thomas Peters coined a concept called "management by wandering around." For you, it may look more like "training by wandering around"—but the idea is the same. Physically walk around and talk to your new teammates. Ask them how things are going, what issues they are having, and how you can help. Back to our newborn example, this is like the new Grandma coming to visit when the baby is born, knowing the new parent has to do the "work," but being there to answer questions, help, and offer support.

For some of the new teammates, they may feel so overwhelmed early on with all of the changes that it may take a number of weeks, or even months, for an understanding of expected usage to really sink in. For others, like advisors, they may be eager to learn—but they simply can't find the time to focus on the systems right out of the gate. *That's okay.* It's not an excuse, but it's a reality you need to be prepared for.

In considering your role, remember that early adoption will either be reinforced or dropped based on your ability to help your new teammates at

---

[2]Peters, T. J., and Waterman, R. H. (2006). *In Search of Excellence: Lessons from America's Best-Run Companies.* Harper Business, New York.

this critical stage. So stay close by, offer helpful reminders, and be flexible to the needs of each person while reinforcing acceptable usage standards. Some may want you within arm's length to answer every little question, but others may not want you hovering overhead.

<u>Ongoing Training</u>
In terms of ongoing training, you want to build off of what you already put together for pre-launch. Hold follow-up sessions each week for the first month, ideally 45 or 60 minutes long. Use the time to reinforce usage expectations and to address any concerns and feedback from the team. Whoever handled the training for your general sessions and your more specific breakouts should do these follow-ups as well.

Gaining buy-in from influencers of the new team is very important, especially since your entity is combined now and it is go-time for usage. If one of your allies can be the one to offer a helping hand during these follow-up sessions, it can go a long way in turning your training into opportunities for successful adoption; resulting in a follow-the-leader effect.

During this phase, be prepared for repetitive questions. You should expect this as it's very normal for people to absorb information at different rates. It takes time for everything to sink in. As stated in the beginning of this chapter, developing good habits make changes more palatable. Repetition is key in making successful adoption a reality. And sometimes that repetition will come from answering the same questions over and over and over.

Be willing to adjust some of your training content as time goes on. You might realize that something didn't turn out according to plan or that everyone is experiencing the same issue that needs to be tweaked. Over the next few months, plan to have plenty of face time with your new team. Whether through onsite visits, one-on-one office hours, or formal training sessions, the ultimate goal is to merge the new team's needs into the overall firm training programs.

Keys to Adoption

Now that your deal is done, you still need to understand the challenges moving forward and prepare to address them head-on.

<u>Leader Reinforcement</u>
At this stage post-close, your job is to help your teammates get used to the new normal. One key to adoption is having high-level firm support from the owners of the business—the ones who made the ultimate decision to bring

these firms together. Now is an important time for these allies to spend time with their staff to listen to their questions, feelings, and concerns, while offering encouragement and appreciation for all of their hard work to make this new venture a success.

Identify a Passionate Sponsor

Matt Mountain and Randy Davis, the men who started NexGen Consultants, are authors of a book on implementing a successful CRM.[3] They talk about the importance of having a passionate sponsor—ideally, a higher-level person in a similar role—to learn the system well and show their colleagues exactly how things can be done. This is a person who will invest a good deal of time, effort, and energy into their people the attitude of "Here, let me show you." We believe this same principle of sponsorship is an effective way to integrate users into new technology and procedures due to a merger or acquisition.

Learning Buddies

Another way to help alleviate the tension inherent to change is to line up every new individual with a Learning Buddy. The purpose of a Learning Buddy is to:

- Keep a connection
- Enhance buy-in from both sides
- Drive ongoing engagement

Chart out each person from "Firm A" and line them up with the appropriate person from "Firm B," and then list out the reason for the pairing. (These do not need to be individuals on your implementation team.) (Table 6.1).

Share the chart with the people in both columns, as well as their managers. This will keep everyone on the same page and is another example of how to have clear and consistent communication.

Since in-person is better than at a distance, ideally, these pairs will be in the same office. You can still pair people up at different locations if needed. However it looks, encourage the buddies to hold regular meetings, phone calls, or even video calls in order to promote the adoption process. You want open communication between Firm A and B in order for each team member to get (or provide) the help needed—as well as the opportunity to ask or answer any questions that arise.

---

[3]Davis, R., and Mountain, M. (2015). *Your Surefire Guide to CRM Success: No More Leaving Money On the Table*. Advantage Media Group, Charleston, SC, p. 102.

Table 6.1 Learning buddies chart

Firm A	Firm B	Reason for pairing
Tara	Chris	Advisors with business development focus
Terry	Carl	Paraplanner responsibilities; both handle marketing items
Todd	Carrie	Client service roles with an emphasis on custodian relations

Incentivized Adoption

As Greg mentioned, some firms may choose to build acceptance and usage of new systems into their compensation. Each individual employee may have goals tied to the changes, such as their usage, ideas for improvements, and their ability to help others. Potentially, there could be incentives for an entire teams' adoption efforts.

Tune In … and Help Them Adjust

Be especially tuned into your new people. Know who is going to be ready to go with the change versus who will be reluctant. Help those change-resistant people dial in, so to speak, by showing the similarities and then also acknowledging the differences. Spend time with them and use language like:

- Here's how it's the same…
- With the exceptions of…

Changing a system is not actually the biggest issue in adoption. Rather, it's the challenge of a person being willing to change their behavior in order to use a new system.

Wild Cards

Although you have a plan for communicating well and training everyone in a way your integration team believes will work, it's unlikely that everything will go according to plan. The following are wild cards you may encounter and how to prepare and respond to them.

Your Own Uncertainty

Let's say you recently went through an adjustment to how your firm handles some procedure—like starting to utilize an electronic signature system, tracking pre-clearance of employee trades through your CRM, or utilizing a new client portal. Since this is a new procedure and somewhat unproven, you may find it hard to put this into your training program. You may feel odd training new members of the firm on something that you can't show them (or even tell) works well, even though the change *is* the right move.

Advice: Keep the new procedure in your training. If the implementation team hasn't changed that technology or process during this merge, don't publicly question your firm's decision to move in this direction. Express your confidence that this direction makes sense; and be mindful of all the reasons why the decision was made in the first place. Be clear that your team thought through taking this route and despite it being a new process or system, it's the future for where the firm is going.

Insufficient Training Before Technology Launch

As we stated earlier, try to conduct 3 to 4 training sessions. To us, this is an ideal number. But the reality is that not everyone will be able to schedule that amount of time with their new counterparts. So, you need to consider: what do I think is the minimum amount of training content required to get my new teammates up and running for Day 1?

Advice: If productivity is the primary focus, then you need to make sure you are preparing each individual for the essentials for daily operations. At a minimum, they need:

- A general understanding of the systems to be used
- General operating procedures for each system
- A training run-through on "a day in the life"

With someone who can't attend all the training sessions, for example a traveling advisor, find out what time they do have pre-launch. Cover the most critical items you can in that window. You can plan for future sessions to go over the general usage again and dive deeper into the departmental items specific to each role. Your availability at launch, along with the implementation team's, will be a critical and sought-after resource for these people who couldn't get more training.

In some cases, a deal might come together so quickly that holding multiple formal training sessions simply isn't feasible. In this case, use what time you have with both teams to discuss the culture of technology and how current systems are used. Have your managers or SMEs spend whatever time is available to do the critical Day 1 training. Have them focus on practical examples, like simulations of the actions a user will need for their role to be functional at launch.

Catering

The question comes up if you should cater to individuals who didn't attend training or simply aren't keeping up with the rest of the group. This isn't bound to happen, but don't be surprised if you have a person or two (especially in larger firms) who might slide by during training without paying attention to the details or not fully understand all aspects of what was covered.

Advice: In the short term, catering to the needs of these individuals is beneficial. You do not want their work to suffer and neither does anyone else on their team (clients, teammates, vendor relationships). To be clear: we find it acceptable to spend extra time with individuals who need it, with the full intention of getting them on board with acceptable usage standards within a specified time period.

Within six months, though, if someone is not up to speed with technology adoption, there could be a larger problem. As you reach this point, we would not advise you to continue catering to their needs. If there was irreparable damage in the working relationship for this individual due to the integration of these two firms, it's up to your managers to evaluate the best course of action, given the ongoing issues.

Someone Wants to Throw in the Towel

We all have them: one, or a series of tough days, when everything seems to be piling up on us and nothing turns out in our favor. It can leave an individual feeling frustrated, overwhelmed, and helpless. Add in a bunch of new systems and procedures and the thought of walking out the front door can look appealing.

Advice: Set up a Go-To person for the new team member to turn to when they need support. These can be:

- *Someone inside their historical circle of trust*: You should task and prepare an existing teammate to offer help, guidance, and encouragement for this individual.
- *Learning buddies*: Hopefully, the relationships you established are doing well, and any new team member has access to their buddy when times get tough.
- *Their trainer*: Instead of ripping their hair out in frustration, screaming, "I NEED HELP" or even "I QUIT!"—make it clearly known from the beginning that the main teacher for particular training content is accessible for questions anytime.

- *Technical help*: It's possible that the problems are technical in nature (ex. data entry, workflow errors with systems usage, or accessibility problems). From training onward, and especially after launch, make sure your people know you've provided technical resources and where to find them.

In your training, include how important it is for an individual to communicate when things aren't going well. To help with this, prepare answers to some FAQs such as:

- Where do I go with questions on:
  - Basic usage
  - Procedures
  - Data issues
  - Access problems
  - Where do I find …

- Where do I go with suggestions?
  - I'd like to see a change …
  - I have an enhancement idea on …

- Where do I go for Technical help?
  - Where is it when I need it?
  - Where/to whom do I go to fix my error?
  - Why isn't this working?

Remind everyone involved to practice healthy and professional habits to get them through stressful moments.

Real-Life Examples

A few of the HIFON firms Shaun spoke to about their M&A experiences shared these tips for adoption:

- *Staff meetings training*: Incorporate reminders and general FAQs in each of your company or departmental meetings. Always take advantage of the opportunity to share a repeated message.
- *Develop written checklists for new procedures*: if you can share documented materials, do so. Some people are simply more comfortable looking up the answer before reaching out to someone. Checklists not only help with

training your current new members, but are a guide for future hires and are helpful in reviewing procedures over time.

- *People learn differently so plan for the group, but be flexible with individuals.* Some may need you to keep your training at a higher level, while others may want the nitty-gritty details. Also, consider ways to make your training effective for visual, audible, and hands-on learners.

Stacey McKinnon, COO of Morton Capital Management in Calabasas, CA, shared some of her thoughts on training for silo advisors joining a larger ensemble firm.

The challenge is: what are they going to plug into? Where does the new advisor fit in? If their book of business is following them in, how do you enhance the relationship with the client to go beyond that advisor?

Often, advisors come from an investment only business. But adding the financial planning side (requiring dual expertise) adds value for the clients. In order to accomplish this training, if you have the capacity, give your new advisor a mid-level advisor or a senior CSA to fully dedicate time to them for 6 months or more.

The formerly siloed advisor may not make much time for formal training, but the support advisor or CSA will essentially handle the technology and the onboarding assignments of teaching, training, and educating the new advisor through their regular meetings. The support advisor or CSA becomes the go-to person, which will not only help the new advisor get up to speed, but alleviates the responsibility for this training from the firm's leadership team.

Although it might be hard for new advisors to let go of former responsibilities, like the trading and rebalancing process, for example, letting their trusted new teammate send those responsibilities to other departments or roles will ultimately free up the advisor for more client time—enhancing the value of their relationships.

Bottom Line with Adoption

- **Trust your gut!**
  One firm admitted they've gone against their best practices before … with regret. They shared how they made an exception to their timing plan, trying to rush things when it wasn't prudent. This can happen if the time of year isn't ideal (ex. tax season). In theory, everything may seem okay and the other firm may be saying there isn't a problem, but trust your instincts for what is the right thing to do. The lesson from this example: delay the expedited timeline in the best interests of the firm in the long run.
- **You can be strict!**
  Sometimes (ahem, often) advisors will want to hold onto their old ways of doing things. If your company doesn't let advisors process anything an administrator or CSA can do, and there's a strong system and process in

place to support them, then stick to it: teach, train, and enforce. It's okay to hold new people to your standards.

- **Repeat as necessary.**
  Early on after launch, it may become clear that the new team hasn't grasped the changes you were teaching them—quarterly reports or client portals, for example. Although there has been ample training, if there are more questions that seem appropriate, this indicates they probably didn't get it. The lesson: as soon as you are aware of the problem areas, bring these items up frequently and repetitively to reinforce learning.

- **There's no way but through.**
  Ever try to feed a toddler a vegetable? You know it's good for them and that they need to eat it, but most kids initially resist. We hate to say this, but in the same way, you have to be okay with an initial "choking and gagging period" as people adjust to changes in the workplace. But just like a child may end up listing broccoli as a favorite food as they get older, it may take upwards of 6–12 months to get people used to new systems. They may still talk about "how we used to do it," but after a year, you should find the entire group is at a new normal. To help, add a regular line item in your staff meeting agenda each month to address suggestions and give feedback. Then it may require a committee to meet regularly to decide what will get priority for updates.

The way your teams will work together over time is dynamic. Be open to adjustments and enhancements as time goes on. Here are some final thoughts from the firms we interviewed.

- *Embrace a culture of adoption*
  One firm we spoke to told us about a highly involved majority share-holder who they knew could have a big impact on the firm moving forward. People on both sides of the deal highly valued, respected, and followed this leader. This top-end buy-in was all it took to drive their culture of adoption. The team understood (and followed) the leader's "gung-ho" attitude about the new direction. In this instance, the team quickly adapted to change in order to be successful.

- *Identify a key operations person from the incoming team*
  Whether time is short or you're bringing in a small team, identify at least one key operations person from the incoming firm. Having this person can make a big difference during adoption. They will be the one to make sure reporting is going to be available, invoicing will be set up correctly, and contacts are ready for marketing. This person, who knows the essentials for launch, is a blessing. If possible, this person would spend more

time up front with your people in order to gain a level of knowledge to carry their team through the early weeks and months after you launch any new technology.

- *Create adoption advancement opportunities*
Along the same lines as above, identify if there are individuals from your firm with the capacity to aid in data management or any other client service need. Use these extra set of (knowledgeable) hands not only to help the migration, but also to advance the new team's adoption. Given the effort of the one side and the willingness to embrace their involvement on the other, it's a great opportunity to bring people together under a common goal.

- *Set realistic expectations for incoming advisors*
Just as your new advisors will be familiarizing their clients with the new platform (custodian statements, performance reporting, etc.) it's important to make sure they are well aware of what will change and be different from their own current environment. You don't want to scare them with too much information or change at once, but prepare them as early as possible in easily digestible chunks. Have a plan for releasing the information in increments through your training. For example:

  - Show them how to access performance and account data, or other frequently referenced information about their clients' accounts.
  - Explain how to track emails and utilize the CRM system so it will help them find the client information, notes, and activities that are important to them.
  - In the midst of internal systems training, familiarize the advisors with what clients will experience with the custodians, such as eDelivery options and online access.

- *Consider the impact on operations and clients*
One firm shared a hard experience of transitioning a single advisor who was bringing over clients. The existing firm felt as though they were speaking a different language than the advisor in terms of systems and servicing requests. This led to a disconnect between understanding the advisor's operations and connecting with the existing firm's operations. Specifically, the implementation team had trouble figuring out the details about custodial accounts, money managers, and which investment platforms were being used.
Obviously, not knowing how many platforms the new advisor had was bad. But trying to figure out how to map their investment accounts and managers into their existing platforms only made it worse. An additional challenge was trying to figure out what was held through the RIA versus the brokerage side of the business.

The advisor was with his previous firm for only a year before transitioning to this new firm, which meant his clients were already fairly new to the investment platforms and custodians. Moving again this soon was a challenge for the ops team to manage.

The benefit of bringing over this advisor ended up paling in comparison to the cost of all the headaches and additional work involved for operations.

- *Accept that you've overturned the apple cart*

Not to be too cliché, but let's face it, you're turning over the apple cart when you change most of someone's major systems. But once people get past the change, it will be fine. Initially, it might take a lot of hand-holding to get people through this phase. So once you know what the problems are, sit down with your new teammates and tackle them one at a time. Be constructive and respond with solutions.

That being said: it is okay if you don't give everyone exactly what they want. There will be times where there simply isn't a work around or any mutually beneficial solutions that will make an individual happy. Support them as necessary, but keep in mind that "the pie chart doesn't have to be red" (i.e., clients may not care as much as the advisors do).

Xandra Pendergrass, COO of Signature Family Wealth Advisors in Norfolk, VA, shared some of her experiences about leading their incoming firm's adoption of "The Signature Way."

To start, Signature assembled a team internally to brainstorm how to approach their entire M&A project. They held meetings twice a week where they set timelines so they knew when decisions had to be made. The group would vary in size, depending on who needed to be there for the topics, departments, and systems being discussed.

Once they had a timeline for when the deal was happening (for them, it happened very quickly—within a month!), they started inviting members of the new firm to their meetings. The goal was to get their input and be champions for their incoming team. It was at this point when Xandra began visiting the new office for these meetings.

At first, although Xandra attended the meetings, she didn't have enough experience with the actual client interaction to know all she needed to be able to train everyone at every level. But she knew enough to identify that the flow of the new team wasn't where it needed to be. She kept saying, "They don't know what to do," meaning that they continued doing things in their own way. She needed more boots on the ground to show them The Signature Way.

Xandra wanted the changes to be real and to encourage a blend of cultures, so she quickly put into place a cultural expectation. She assigned someone from Signature to be in the new office (which was reasonably close by) Monday through Thursday of each week. She created a calendar for other members of the Signature team to visit the new team regularly, which worked out well. She wanted to make sure someone from the existing team was available for simple questions and to show them The Signature Way, live in person.

To be clear, the group did have a lot of system changes: Outlook contacts had to migrate to their version of Microsoft Dynamics CRM; performance reporting was changing from balance sheets generated out of QuickBooks to transactions flowing through Tamarac's Advisor View; their old way of encrypting emails was left behind and joined Signature's use of Zix; and new document storage would exist through Sharefile.

With a fair amount of encouragement and even some pushing to get full adoption of these new systems, Xandra's efforts worked out well as the new group adopted The Signature Way.

Key Takeaways

Our goal in this chapter has been to guide you through the process of adoption leading up to and, most importantly, after you launch new technology. From preparation for culture and technology changes, to how building trust is a key to success, by using examples and the experiences of others, we want to equip and prepare you for managing successful adoption at your firm.

The goal of technology adoption is not just usage, but *effective* usage. We don't just want our teams to use the new systems, we want them to use the technology well. We want our people to excel at what they do because of our supportive technology choices.

You've heard the idiom "you catch more flies with honey than with vinegar" and this holds true for the basic principles of adoption as well.

Don'ts (Vinegar)

- Don't communicate with vague phrasing, using vague timelines
- Don't use harsh words
- Don't expect the entire new staff to "get it" on the first pass
- Don't shame or embarrass people for asking questions you think they should already know the answer to
- Don't be patronizing or condescending if a staff member doesn't know how to do a certain task and is coming to you for help
- Don't create an environment where people are afraid to ask questions
- Don't offer training via an outdated manual handed out on Day 1 (Or worse: A nonexistent or intentionally bare-bones training)

Do's (Honey)

- Do value relationships and strive to work well together
- Do make efforts across the board to build key allies
- Do communicate frequently, clearly, and openly about timelines and acceptable usage standards

- Do your best to show empathy
- Do offer well thought out training which is flexible enough to adjust to the nuances of the team and how it has operated in the past
- Do encourage openness and clarity

As your firm works itself through this adoption process, your sights will quickly be looking onward toward additional successes, carried on by your current momentum. And this leads us into the next topic we take up in the following chapter on growth.

Greg's Final Word

Implementation of new technology may seem like a finish line, and though it's certainly an achievement, you're really just getting started. All of the time, money and hard work you've invested up until now—assessing, researching, strategizing, and building relationships between firms to ensure a smoother transition—is really just the first half of the process. Adoption can be a challenge on many levels and as a leader you need to do your part to help shepherd people through what I call the three "E's"—enthusiasm, efficiency, and example.

Your responsibility is to be excited about new systems and processes and to encourage that excitement in others. You also need to promote efficient behavior that empowers people to always think in terms of streamlining these new processes. Lastly, it's not enough to be a cheerleader—you must show your team that you're walking the walk by learning at the very least the basic structure and usage for your systems.

7

Next Steps and Growing Forward Together

First of all, take a moment to congratulate yourself and your team on how far you've come. Often, we don't sit still long enough to look back at our accomplishments and recognize those who did the heavy lifting to get us there. Take a deep breath and enjoy the moment. Go out for dinner as a team. Pop some champagne. Celebrate!

As you settle in to your new normal, be careful that you don't settle! The real work is just beginning. This is a perfect time to realign and communicate—and communicate again—your firm's strategic objectives and benchmarks for growth. And while things don't need to change overnight or even in the near future, it's important to keep in mind that success today does not ensure success tomorrow. It's a never-ending process of regularly assessing your technology every few years from a service perspective. That's not to say that this is "bad" news or "good" news for the business—it's simply where we as advisors need to live to stay competitive in an ever-changing market. There is some legitimate "good" news to take away, though, and it's that you've proven that when your people can perform at capacity with your technology, procedures, and have integrated well in terms of culture, you've laid an excellent foundation for additional growth.

In this final chapter, I'll discuss how leaders can capitalize on momentum and use that to set goals for the future. Then Shaun will share his thoughts on how the team can think about forward progress and plan for the next phase together.

© The Author(s) 2018
G. Friedman and S. Kapusinski, *The Financial Advisor M&A Guidebook*,
https://doi.org/10.1007/978-3-030-00003-5_7

What Success Looks Like

Needless to say, a successful technology integration looks different in every situation and depends on what matters to the firm and its people. I'll tell you that there is no bullseye or magical formula for success, but there are certainly elements that you want to see working seamlessly in the business and people who are satisfied and proud to be a part of the new team. For Private Ocean, those elements are fairly simple and perhaps have more to do with its cultural impact than a technology one. Success for us means that we're all working on common systems, our processes are integrated (or intentionally not integrated) and there are no longer two sides. No "us" and "them," no "their way" and "our way," just one voice across locations and teams working forward without getting tangled in the details. That didn't happen quickly, of course, and it took great effort and patience on everyone's part around language, around how to overcome the invisible challenges of multiple offices, and to take time to understand new and different perspectives and still keep the end goal in mind of serving our clients. And frankly it is a never fully ending process—it moves from a "major lifting" project to more of a "constant assessment and improvement" process.

Now, if your goal is to silo offices and keep things separate, success will look a little different. But within our business model, our goal was to centralize operations with a home office and satellite offices and to present a unified brand where our clients could land in any branch and have a consistent experience.

No matter your situation, success boils down to efficiency, continued momentum, engaged employees, and happy clients. It's important to keep in mind that success is a moving target and it takes a consistent and persistent effort to collaborate, communicate, and explore new paths to growth. I encourage teams to meet offsite periodically to realign goals, nurture your common bond and sense of community, and tie everything back to your firm's mission.

Also recognize and accept that during your next M&A event, you'll likely make different mistakes and find new challenges to address. There's an old adage that when it comes to a merger or acquisition and I've mentioned it in previous chapters: Your first year should be focused on alignment and building structure which sets you up for the second year and profitability. I've used that in my mindset with our mergers to set expectations, and with our most recent transition we've seen a lot of progress at about the 7-month mark. Staying true to your vision and strategy and following the steps outlined in this book will help minimize your odds for disruption and help keep you on track to achieving your own success.

Measuring Success

If identifying success wasn't nebulous enough, measuring it can seem even more abstract. With technology, specifically your CRM platform, there are certain efficiencies you can capture over time to determine if your integration is working or not working. The outcome may mean reallocating resources, investing in more training in certain areas, or streamlining workflows that haven't quite made the impact that you intended. True business success is about understanding, monitoring and having good metrics, but that is a discussion for another book!

How we measure success post-adoption is by establishing an "Acceptable Usage Standard," or the basic level of technology usage we expect everyone in the firm to meet consistently. For each relevant system used in a specific role, we expect users to be able to complete basic tasks and follow processes that allow us to capture data that can be used to measure efficiency and progress. All it takes is one or two people not using your systems properly to impact the efficiency of a system, and with regular monitoring you'll be able catch any issues before they start impacting the firm.

Let me kick things over to Shaun here for his insight into measuring success related to metrics as well as how to create an effective 100-day integration plan.

Key Performance Indicators (KPIs) in Measuring Success

Many factors can impact your firm's success metrics related to technology, including adding or losing employees and clients and upgrades to technology. To address these factors, consider the following:

- Employees need ongoing training and to be cared for as key assets of the firm
- Clients need to be communicated with about upcoming changes, and listened to for feedback, as those changes occur
- Successful usage of the firm's technology plays a significant role in how efficiently your team carries out the activities needed to satisfy your firm's objectives, from managing client's money to handling their planning needs

Mistakes, missteps, or mismanagement of any of these areas can be costly and time consuming. Ultimately, they will impact the performance and growth trajectory of your firm.

In order to keep an objective pulse on your growth progress, we encourage you to watch your KPIs. The following is a list[1] provided from Michael Kitces on typical metric items to measure:

- Firm metrics
  - Gross revenue
  - Direct expenses
  - Overhead expenses
  - Gross profit margin
  - Net/operating profit margin

- Growth
  - New amount/percentage of revenue from new clients
  - New amount/percentage of revenue from existing clients
  - Percent of recurring revenue
  - Client retention rate
  - Revenue (or asset) retention rate

- Clients
  - Average revenue/client
  - Distribution of revenue/client
  - Distribution (and average) of client age
  - Distribution of revenue (or revenue/client) by client age
  - Client revenue/hour
  - Profit/client

This is by no means an exhaustive list. Certainly, your firm keeps other financial or operational KPIs. But these are examples of data you should watch, measure, and analyze over time to track your firm's progress.

You might also consider revisiting any benchmarking studies your firm participated in in the past. If you can take part again, see how the results change over time. The results are not the only measurements you'll use to determine success. But, it's another source of information to drive change (technology or otherwise) toward your firm's strategic objectives.

---

[1]Kitces, M. (2014) *What Are The Key Performance Indicators (KPIs) for Your Financial Planning Firm?* Kitces.com. Accessed 1 August 2018.

Five Questions for Advisors Assessing New Technology

When it comes to new technology, advisors sometimes experience a nagging paranoia that they're missing out on the next big thing. Every day it seems, we are inundated with the latest, greatest application—a shiny new tech tool that if you were to believe the marketers, will revolutionize how we do business.

With all the lightning-fast marketing enhancements to technology, it's difficult to know what train to board and which application that's supposed to save hours of time is just a flash in the pan. The good news is that reliable leads on new tools can come from anywhere—publications, conferences, tech experts, peers, and employees. The not-so-good news is that there are so many options to choose from that it can be overwhelming and time-consuming to investigate.

So how can advisors cut through the sales noise and really assess whether or not the latest tech is the *greatest* tech—or more importantly the RIGHT tech for your firm? Here are my (Greg) top 5 questions that I ask to make both a swift decision and avoid missing out on a potentially useful new system.

1. **Does it make sense to our business?** Are you trying to add services, streamline operations, add efficiencies, or solve a problem? What is your business case for pursuing this technology, and is it compelling enough to disrupt operations to integrate it into your firm?
2. **Where can I learn more (objectively)?** Sure, you'll visit the company's website and even listen to a sales pitch. But do your homework and seek out objective resources. Often, I find great information about technology from conferences, user groups, respected publications like *InvestmentNews*, and from industry experts like Joel Bruckenstein at *Technology Tools for Today*.
3. **Do they have a demo or test site?** During the sales demo, come prepared to ask questions that are specific to you. This isn't a test but rather an exercise of both the tool and the knowledge of its people. Beyond the sales demo, see if there is a version of the application that you can actually test with your data in your office.
4. **How does this tech "play" nicely with my existing technology?** Chances are, you've already invested quite a bit into your existing technology suite. It's important to understand from the beginning if this new application offers integrations with your current programs.
5. **What would integration look like?** If you're feeling confident that you've found a system that may work for you, start to give some thought to how you would integrate it into your current operations. Consider what your roadmap might look like and how easy or difficult it might be to implement. Sometimes the tool might be useful, but the timing is off.

We've all been dazzled by shiny objects when it comes to making our businesses more efficient. That's not necessarily unique to our industry. What's different is that many of us are smaller operations where everyone wears many hats; even mid-sized and larger firms operate at high levels of capacity. We believe we have mastered the art of running lean, mean, client-service machines, and the allure of technology is understandably strong when it promises to save us resources and elevate our growth.

And while it may not always make sense to hit the brakes every time a new technology claims it will change your business, it's helpful to keep a watchful eye open to ensure that you don't miss out on something that could actually make an impact (Table 7.1).

Table 7.1 A quick due diligence checklist for choosing new technology

Q.	A.
How long has the vendor been in business?	This is not a knock on newer firms, it's just important to know what you're working with. Longevity often means stability, history and reputation. Other things to consider—Are they a private or public company? How is ownership laid out? Who are their leaders?
What is their vision?	Who are they serving? What is their mission? Why do they do what they do? Does it align with your firm's values and goals?
What does their roadmap look like?	What milestones are they using for the future? Where are they headed and what do they hope to achieve in 12 months? 24 months? 5 years?
How many customers do they have?	Are they a larger operation or more "mom and pop?" More importantly, how many customers do they have *like you?*
What's their support model?	What is their capacity for serving their clients and how do they communicate in general? What can your expectations be when you need assistance and training?
Where can you learn about their security?	Ask to see their security language. What steps are they taking to protect your data and your client's data? What backups are in place in case of an issue?

Note: Don't just take a vendor's word for their service—ask for references. I recommend speaking to at least three other customers and you may not necessarily find these referrals from the company itself. Instead, ask around for honest feedback from your peers or a network like HIFON. You may also find former customers who are willing to share why they ended the relationship. Setting expectations early, based on as much information as you can gather, can only be beneficial for your business

Roadmap 101: Creating a 100-Day Integration Plan

When I (Shaun) was younger, my dad took a sabbatical from his teaching position and arranged some speaking events across the country. Instead of driving through the night, stopping only for gas and coffee refills in order to get to the next event, our family of five traveled in a yellow VW van from our home in the Midwest along what felt like a circuitous route—to places like Mt. Rushmore in South Dakota, Yellowstone National Park in Wyoming, and the Grand Canyon in Arizona.

As an adult now, I realize that my dad's events were only part of the reason we went on that trip. My parents wanted to show us the varied landscape of our country that summer. Each stop was extremely intentional and on purpose. And as eager as we were to arrive somewhere new, the five of us tumbling out of the car, stretching our legs—taking pictures and maybe even staying a night or two, we always—always—ended up getting back into the van to keep going.

The life of your business is similar to a cross country trip. As you get to one of your "destinations" along the way, you cross a major item off your list. It's significant. Get out of the car and enjoy the view. But in order to get to all the places you want to go, you can't just stay there. You need to move on and you need a map to get you there. There's no need to rush unnecessarily, but grab a cup of coffee, program the GPS, and hit the road again. You've got more ground to cover.

Similarly, if you are in a growth mindset, one strategy is to have a 100-day integration plan—a road map—visible to all for what will happen in the first 100 days post close. It will be a detailed plan to support all the work done in the previous 180 (or so) days.

It should include engagement with all of your new teammates, assessment of their connection to the new firm's direction, and consideration for what tools and data are necessary to make the goals of the deal come to fruition. You'll tap into system functionality such as daily usage and data reports to show information is being entered. The output should line up with your stated goals, always centered around your acceptable usage standards for each role in the firm.

Keep in mind, deal fatigue is a possibility. One part of your brain feels as if you've crossed the finish line and you'd like to slow down or stop; but the other part knows nothing is really slowing down—it's simply time for the next phase to begin. A 100-day integration plan will help you to stay engaged post-close to drive adoption, get your team up to speed, and set yourself up for additional growth.

An excellent strategy for a firm to excel post-acquisition is to identify a true advocate for the 100-day integration plan. You want someone who not only understands where the company is going, but lives and breathes it each and every day. This person has the breadth of knowledge to help make it happen—either through delegation, training, or their own self-will. This person will be positioned to broadly communicate the successes of the combined firm in real time. They will be able to keep a broad view of what's being accomplished alongside the checklist of what still needs to happen. Depending on the size and scope of your company, the best person for this job could be you.

Future Technology Goals, Future Growth

Beyond integration, you may have already set goals for the future of your firm's technology. Some of these goals might include items like the following:

- Limiting advisors time spent in your trading and rebalancing system
- Moving all training into a learning management system
- Providing clients access to a completely digital onboarding experience
- Giving advisors full mobile access and capabilities to your systems

To get you to these goals, which we all know won't happen naturally on their own, you're going to need a strategic plan.

Similar to a 100-day M&A technology integration plan, if your firm does not have this already, we highly recommend making a technology roadmap for the future. By setting your sights on your firm's growth objectives from a technology perspective, your operations and technology team will be highly involved in identifying what it will take to execute these goals. By following a map and sticking to your targeted destinations, your firm will continue to move toward continued growth, especially if you can avoid the pitfalls of getting off course.

Don't Get Lost!

Avoid these common errors to help your firm stay on the right road for technology growth and success.

1. *Getting lost in the daily maintenance.* You can stay plenty busy putting out fires and keeping everyone happy with what you have—and this is important work! But if you don't have resources to go beyond this daily maintenance work, you're going to fall behind.
2. *Not putting enough leadership behind your goals.* You need a technology leader to drive the execution of the firm's stated technology objectives. They need to be supported by the firm's top leadership and fully empowered to engage vendors, enter into contracts, and drive change.
3. *Failing to hold your implementation leader accountable.* It's on your firm's top executives to put this tech leader into place and to work with this person on a budget toward aligning the firm's tech spend with your primary objectives. Results will dictate the evaluation of their efforts and your top brass has the role of rewarding or reworking based on the outcomes.

How Success Leads to Growth

A successful transition of your technology not only positions the firm well for integrating its new team members, but also for the next wave of technology enhancements. Going into Day 1, everyone knew what was expected of them and it didn't take long for someone to figure out what it looked like when they hit or missed the mark.

Although there probably was a dip in productivity, as people learned new systems, the goal was to see each and every person successfully make the transition to get everyone past proficiency and into mastery. The purpose, ultimately, is so the firm can focus on its next growth strategies.

From launch and into the months that follow, you have been instilling confidence in your current and new team by being able to move data, merge systems, and integrate all users onto one platform. Use the communication muscles you've built up in this process leading up to this point to actively share the successes happening all around the firm. This is especially important to show leaders who have joined you. When leaders buy in, they help drive the speed of both adoption and interest in future technology growth decisions.

Lessons on Success from HIFON Firms

- *The benefits of physical proximity.* One firm made a physical change on top of their systems changes when their deal closed. They moved office locations almost immediately in order to bring everyone together in one spot, and included some room to grow. They felt that "coming together" was a success because as people began to interact both professionally and personally, they clearly saw the groups' cultures merge together in a positive fashion. In addition, helping hands were physically nearby when someone needed help with a new system. Growth firms don't wait until they're bursting at the seams to make these kinds of moves.
- *When you're thrown into the ocean, you quickly learn to build a boat.* One firm shared an unforeseen benefit of going through an M&A event together: their teams got better.

  They knew it would be a lot of work, but both groups quickly responded when they initially heard about their upcoming transition. Since they didn't have time to hem-and-haw, they got right to asking "What's the plan?" and "Who is doing what?" You won't grow together if you're not ready to work together.

Because of their tight timeline, both sides bonded together even before the close of the deal. They learned lessons about themselves as individual leaders as well as the rest of their team (new and existing). This event did expose some weaknesses, which they could work on after the deal's close, but it also identified previously unrecognized strengths. It felt like the options were sink or swim, so everyone worked together to make it a success.

- *The importance of graciousness.* Some firms operate and execute as a planning and investment team with near perfection. It's like a well-oiled machine. But when you start to work on your first M&A deal, it's usually anything but well-oiled. In fact, it can feel clunky and look like it's barely holding on at times. Although we all know that you learn more by making mistakes, the problem is that no one ever wants to make them! Culturally, one firm can unknowingly apply pressure on the other to get everything right. Certainly, this expectation is a hindrance to growth.

  Firms can actually stunt their growth when they've dialed their processes in so tight that there is no room for error or even suggestions. So, encourage a culture that is flexible and gracious. Don't make people afraid to let you know there needs to be a change. We all want everything to go smoothly. As a group, be open to new ideas and be understanding if your initial plan of transition doesn't work out as well as everyone wanted it to on the first try. Without this type of cultural adjustment, you just might stunt your own development.

Enhancement for Growth

Transitioning into a new firm and into new technology is challenging, even painful at first. It can feel like the Day 1 functionality is remarkably less than what it should be. But after your new teammates get through that uncomfortable initial adoption period, things do get easier. The comfort level increases. And that's when you start looking to the future and can start leading everyone toward increased development and growth of your systems going forward.

Consistency

In the months following a technology launch, it's important to continue to talk through integration of the working cultures. You may notice, through the use of systems and even your client service styles, that not everyone works the same way. Address even the smallest differences as quickly and definitively as possible.

Terms, words, and language need to line up and should be consistent across the firm. This isn't a power trip: your goal is simply to provide your advisors and clients with a reliable and replicable experience.

One way to address these differences is to share case studies and stories of client and advisor situations that truly exemplify the outcomes you'd like to see. By relating to a familiar situation, it can help your team understand the purpose and benefits of consistency, especially looking into the future.

Training

You need to commit to ongoing technology training as a long-term objective for your firm. You want training that is organized and well thought out. If your firm currently has poor systems training for the existing team today, and you'd like to avoid additional challenges for the future, focus on improving through the following action items:

- Rework how you handle new hire training, making use of SMEs for initial and ongoing training sessions
- Devise a timeline for follow-up training at 30 days from initial hire, then another session at 60 days, and once you hit 90 days their training should line up with all full-time employees training
- All firm employees should have regularly scheduled training sessions on your systems no less often than quarterly, if not something small each month
- Develop and share documentation at initial training for your employees to use as a reference tool for common and repetitive questions, and update FAQs based on session feedback and system enhancements

A note of advice—don't wait for an M&A event to work on improving your firm's training experience. If you've already gone through it, we're sure you have a good idea of what parts of the training need to be refined. And if you haven't gone through it yet, we encourage you to proactively prepare. It's a process that only benefits the company in the long run.

Operations Leadership

As your firm grows through merger or acquisition, the lead operations roles will remain vital to continued growth. Why? Because as each firm evolves over time, operations roles play a big part in keeping the technology doing what it should and handling responses to the team's and client's current needs.

If the staff experiences any issues, errors, or other tech problems, operations leads are often the ones responsible. Ops leads also manage the expectations for enhancements. It's the ops lead who gets asked, "Can I get it to do X or Y?" and "how soon can we make that change?"

What can happen, though, is the challenge of getting caught up in the maintenance aspect of your current systems. People like to get—and stay—comfortable. Ops leads are there to clearly drive technology improvement initiatives into the future.

You may run into a challenge with keeping silo systems, where data is locked up (no integration or use outside of that program), or using spreadsheets instead of systems that don't work well with the current technology stack. As you institutionalize processes that were once manual or that lacked transparency, work toward adopting a common philosophy of operating with technology going forward.

It's important that this philosophy is shared across your firm, making sure everyone understands the direction. Your technology roadmap is the tool for connecting your firm's tech philosophy with your firm's future desired state. Once the stage is set, the operations leader and the operations team can execute on those decisions.

We want to be clear, existing system maintenance is extremely important. And performance needs to keep up with the expectations you've set—whether for new employees on existing systems or on a new system altogether. But as time passes, avoid getting entangled with short-term perfection on current usage by each and every employee. You want the ability to look ahead and to see the big picture of growing your tech offering beyond where it sits today.

We know that growth by adding new people also brings challenges. An operations lead will try their best to keep everyone happy, while knowing the limits of what's actually possible.

Keep in mind: you can't make 100% of the people happy 100% of the time with your systems and their capabilities. In fact, if you try to make even a few people 100% happy, you'll end up spending so much time on them, your major roadmap improvement items are likely to fall behind. So shoot for 100% of the team being 80% pleased, 100% of the time.

Future M&A Transactions

For a firm who is contemplating growth through M&A, the strategy may include plans for multiple transactions over time. Here are some questions a firm may ask:

Are we fully prepared to handle another M&A, now that we've gone through one?
Every M&A event you go through better prepares you for the next one, whether your next transaction is acquiring a single advisor without any staff or merging with a firm that has multiple advisors with a few staff members each.

But the honest, short answer is "No." No group is ever fully prepared to handle every unforeseen detail that might arise in your next M&A transaction. That being said, we hope this book will help you believe you will do an even better job the next time.

Will our next M&A be similar to the one we just went through?
Like people, each event has its own personality. Some are easier to deal with than others, but no two transactions are alike. Again, the short answer is no. The silver lining here is that with every new transaction, you get to guide the process. It's a "build your own playbook" type of thing, custom to the event's unique integration needs.

Also, firms change over time, especially after each deal takes place. You now have new people and possibly new technology. There have been adjustments in everything from cultural practices to procedural standards of client service. From training, to language, to expectations—your firm is different. So is your next M&A event.

How are we better prepared than last time, then?
Because now you have more experience. You have learned what went well and what didn't. You learned what it felt like when things went smoothly, and you held onto your seat when it did not. You know what you want to repeat and you've made note of things to avoid.

One HIFON firm chooses to avoid starting with any new software that won't integrate with software they already have. In the past, this wasn't their policy. But after learning the hard way, when they dealt with the effects of non-integrating software, they felt it was a mistake for their firm in the future. Now, it's a non-negotiable.

Are we more attractive as a firm for those looking to join us?
Yes. Your prior experience is attractive as a growth firm. But it's more than just going through the event. It's your proven ability to take over and merge major investment operations areas, like trading, document management, and invoicing. Your success is what gives you an advantage.

In the process of transitioning to one entity, you've also added experience maximizing the efficiency gains coming from merging two independent firms. You've benefited from the combination of small business operations in areas such as IT, marketing, compliance, HR, and accounting. By centralizing all operations, you may seriously boost profit margin potential—this, too, is highly attractive.

A HIFON firm (which we'll call "Firm A") shared ways in which they improved from one deal to the next. In their first M&A transaction, Firm A was the group coming into an existing Firm B. Firm A noticed that although people at both of the firms were actively using similar technology, there wasn't a technology project lead to actively unite them together in usage and procedure. Firm B did not have super users who could optimize the systems and the training that resulted was subpar. Firm A felt like no one from Firm B knew how to use their systems to capacity and that there was a firm-wide lack of consistency.

After Firm A became integrated, and the new entity began looking at additional growth through another acquisition, the leaders from Firm A shared ways their own transition could have been better. So before the second deal even happened, the combined firm invested into listening and improving upon Firm A's experience. Their leadership wanted to empower the entire team to be involved in making this next deal's implementation a success.

In addition, Firm A made sure more tools would be provided to the newest people coming in through training, super user involvement, and detailed communications of their documented procedures. Because of the challenges Firm A faced coming in, they understood ways to improve the process for their future M&A events.

The Impact of Debriefing

Initially, ask everyone involved on the implementation team to spend time reviewing and evaluating the process from the start of their involvement. Shortly after Day 1, within a month or two, start to gather feedback from your implementation team. Make sure you capture their thoughts on what went according to plan and what needed improvement.

Next, conduct internal interviews with individuals who joined into your firm and experienced some of the most change during the implementation phase. You want to talk with the people who now have new ways of doing things. This is best done 3–6 months after you implement technology to allow some time for the dust to settle and for new routines to be established.

Communications: Ask about adequacy, thoroughness, and effectiveness of the communications leading up to Day 1. Was there enough? Too much/too little? How was the quality? Did they feel prepared? Were there any missing pieces?

Training: Did the initial trainings adequately prepare them? What worked well? What didn't? Did they feel there were required sessions that weren't useful? Did they wish they had additional training? If so, on what?

Experiences: How did the actual experience of the transition line up with the expectations that were set ahead of time? Did they feel the expectations were clear and thorough? Were there any unexpected aspects to their role that they weren't prepared for?

Finally, it will be helpful for advisors with clients who experienced some changes to be asked about how they felt throughout the whole process. Ask for feedback on how the process went for the advisors. Do they have any suggestions for improvements?

Debriefing doesn't need to be done through a survey, but you should document your findings. It can be gathered formally through specific meetings. Or it can also be very informal—through casual conversations where you ask if there were changes that had a positive or negative impact on their experiences with your firm.

From here, make a list of Takeaway Do's and Don'ts for future reference. These should center around technology, culture merging, and team integration.

- What was positive and helpful?
- What turned out well?
- What systems or procedures were missed or forgotten?
- What was the thing(s) that bit you in the back-side that you can't miss next time?

Wild Cards

What if an influential manager leaves the firm during or shortly after your M&A event?

Your people and their ability to utilize systems and tools are extremely valuable. So whether it's due to an exciting new opportunity or unfortunate dissatisfaction, if an influential member of your leadership team leaves the firm, it will inhibit the firm's progress of growth. Inevitably, it breaks continuity and adds short-term chaos.

After promoting or hiring someone to take this position, initially, a drop in productivity is to be expected. The individual needs some time to get up to speed and learn how to lead the team in the new direction after the M&A event. This delay isn't catastrophic, but it can cause a shift in the firm's timeline for growth.

So rely heavily on existing management to flag your key people before the transition happens. Highlight them early and address any specific training, buy-in, or cultural issues as soon as possible—on both sides of the deal. Your firm needs these people in order to stay on track with your growth strategy.

What if a role needs to change significantly?

One firm shared the challenges of finding the perfect fit for a great employee, especially when some of their role initially appeared to overlap with another's. For this example, a COO from the incoming firm was the primary go-to for almost anything that needed to be accomplished and virtually all decisions that needed to be made. But the acquiring firm was quiet about the plan for this employee up front, simply because at that time, they didn't understand how valuable he was to the incoming firm.

As his abilities and worth became clear, despite the firm eliminating his former COO role, the firm was intentional in developing a personal path for growth for him within the company. Once this happened, the acquiring firm began to communicate to the rest of the team where this person would fit in the new entity.

What do we do about the things we got wrong or that didn't go well?

First of all, don't view that work as wasted time. It's good to aim for big accomplishments. Sometimes pushing for more to get done in a short amount of time is what you need to do. Even if it all doesn't get done in time, you can still learn from the experience.

Let's say you wanted to implement your rebalancer software across both firms right after your deal closes but the pre-work didn't get finished in time. Or you tried to update all of their client files into your folder structure, but you ran out of time. *It's okay!* You were making progress and can implement it when the time is right; or when the bugs are figured out, and everyone in leadership is on board with the decision to move forward.

Is it a hit to morale or your foundation of trust? Maybe a little bit. But in addition to the actual accomplishment, you also want to build loyalty to the firm and to each other within the process. Some people may jump to conclusions on how far this apparent "miss" might set you back, but don't let a slowdown derail your designed intentions for optimal system integration.

Can we do an M&A transaction again?

Yes, you can always do another deal. It will go best if you take what you've learned during your first deal and commit to improving the process of moving systems and data. After going through the steps of due diligence, a systems and data inventory, and the assessment process, you will have an idea of how prepared you are to tackle those items a second (or third, or fourth) time.

Make sure you answer:

- Were there major risk areas you missed or didn't spend enough time on?
- Should we consider hiring a consultant to figure out some major needs next time?
- Does the firm have the right people resources to lead the project of another deal?

You may not have perfect answers for these questions, but most entrepreneurs want to grow and are willing to take some risks along the way.

Key Takeaways

- Recognize that you, your people, and your business never stop growing. As you continue to assess your technology, look for natural "Champions" who can help keep you updated on the latest tech trends and new releases.
- As your firm strives for realignment with goals and objectives post launch, be sure to keep a pulse of your objective KPIs and benchmarking study results.
- Use the momentum you've built up to your deal's close to push toward growing your technology stack using a road map with a 100-day implementation plan.
- Much of your firm's achievement in this transition will come out of how you frame what success looks like once the deal is done.
- Accept that the planning and execution may not be perfect, but allow for new voices and ideas to break the norms for continued success.
- You may be faced with challenges after completing an M&A technology transition, where it can feel like you're moving backwards before you're moving forward.
- Share case studies of internal successes to help your teams better understand each other.
- Prepare your firm today for future M&A deals by establishing training methods that will work beyond those for new employees; establish ongoing sessions once the deal goes live.
- Work with your key operations staff to drive your technology roadmap to go beyond the typical maintenance of existing systems. Look toward enhancements that will drive firm growth.
- Move forward as a group, not just behind closed doors with other leaders. Private Ocean has a tech committee with a representative from every area

of the company. Everyone has a vested interest in helping the business and offering our clients the best possible experiences. We hold demos all the time, attend conferences, and subscribe to all the main industry publications.

- For future M&A deals, document notes of your integration process by gathering feedback from all parties—from those actively executing the integration plan to those impacted by all of the technology changes.

Greg's Final Word

In previous chapters we have emphasized how change impacts everyone during an M&A event and seems to multiply when it comes to integrating technology across multiple firms. As a leader, it's important to recognize, anticipate and embrace inevitable and constant change as your new firm moves forward. I read something recently that really resonated with me on the subject, from an article in a magazine from therapist and speaker Connie Podesta.[2]

> Change is what makes life exciting, daring, different, inspired. Stop fighting it. Embrace it!

That attitude perfectly sums up how I feel about change. I believe that change shouldn't be perceived as negative, but rather a necessary and important path to improvement. The journey to get there might be a little scary at times and exhilarating at others, but the goal is to constantly evolve and grow—personally and professionally. Those who know me often remind me that I get physically restless and nervous when things tend to stay the same for too long. Call me battle-worn (another word for "experienced," or perhaps technology tested), but the impetus for change has always been unpredictable … and yet inevitable.

Of course, this is not a new topic! Change, and how challenging it can be to process and accept, has been researched, studied, and discussed in countless scientific reports, best-selling books, articles, speeches, and more. For example, the "motivational business fable," *Who Moved My Cheese? An Amazing Way to Deal with Change in Your Work and in Your Life*, by Spencer Johnson,[3] is often considered the ground-breaking guidebook for dealing with change and its benefits on the individual and the business overall.

[2]Podesta, C. (2010) *10 Ways to Stand Out From The Crowd*. Triple Nickel Press, Bloomington, IN.
[3]Johnson, S. (1998) *Who Moved My Cheese? An Amazing Way to Deal with Change in Your Work and in Your Life*. G.P. Putnam's Sons, New York.

Chances are, you've read the book, nodded your head in agreement, and felt inspired by its message.

So why is change so hard? Because we become comfortable with what we already know. Because many of us feel our repeated successes came from following a certain formula to get there. There may have been bumps along the way and lessons learned, but we feel confident in our current paths. It's predictable. It's easy. This is how we've always done something, and it's worked for us so far.

While all of those statements may be true, it's also a big trap. When you deflect change in favor of "what got us here still works," you don't know how fast and how far you're falling behind until you look up and realize you've been outpaced, outperformed, and left in the antiquated dust. Playing catch-up can be painful, costly, and time-consuming.

I'm not saying that overcoming the fear and apprehension over change is easy—if it was there wouldn't be so much written on the subject. But after 35 years of owning two companies and handling a lifetime of business issues and challenges, here are just a few tips I have learned.

- **Breathe.** Take your time with that. Tell yourself that change is not always easy. It's unfamiliar, awkward, and in many cases, it means you have to rely on new people in new ways. It makes you feel vulnerable. All of that is okay to say out loud. Just remind yourself that every step counts and moves you forward toward your goals.
- **Have faith.** Believe that things will turn out well regardless of inevitable bumps in the road. Have confidence that no matter what you run into in changing things that you and your staff will be able to handle things well. By the way, this is a CRITICAL leadership quality! Nobody wants to have a leader that lacks optimism, confidence, and positivity!
- **Expect to be surprised, so that you're not surprised.** Expect that along the way there will be things you hadn't considered or anticipated. Plan for those surprises, so that they're easier to manage.
- **Finally, if things don't turn out as expected (as in well)—find the lemonade in the lemons!** Find the benefits of the "failure"—there are ALWAYS great learnings and benefits, even if not immediately obvious, to changes that don't turn out as planned.

Change does make life exciting, like Connie Podesta said, and it's for better or worse depending on how you approach it. It's what creates new ideas, creates success. Keeping that forward-thinking mentality is both infectious and inspiring—not just for yourself but for those you influence. All you need to do is take that first daring, different, and inspired step.

Afterword by Shaun Kapusinski

Just after I started in the RIA industry in 2003, our firm entered a corporate relay for Akron's inaugural marathon. Our president wanted the firm to be involved in the city's big event, so, eager to make a good impression, I volunteered to be on the team. At the time, there were only 10 people at the company and the relay required five participants. I was young, green, and even though I wasn't a runner, it was clear I should step up. Which was fine—I mean, how hard could running a few miles be?

In a flash, my colleagues claimed the shorter distances of the relay. "Okay someone's gotta run eight." My heart dropped. "Shaun? Shaun, you can run eight miles, right?" I took a deep breath, smiled and nodded with an enthusiastic *Sure!* But in my head, alarm bells rang. I'd always been pretty athletic, but I'd never run farther than a mile.

For my first "training session," I decided to do laps around the parking lot of our apartment complex after work. I put on basketball shorts and a cotton t-shirt, thinking I'd be fine in the 80-degree heat. My wife kissed me and wished me luck. Five minutes in, I was bent over, sucking air, and wincing from the cramp in my side. I hadn't even finished one full mile.

Defeated, I walked back home. "Well, that was quick," my wife laughed. I realized that if I was going to do this—and not make a fool of myself or lose my job—I'd need to rethink my training. I decided I'd make the big goal into smaller goals. My new plan was simply to run one more lap each day than I had the previous day.

I continued to prepare for the marathon relay and thrived within the discipline of the training. I started to read books on running and visited

G. Friedman and S. Kapusinski, *The Financial Advisor M&A Guidebook*,
https://doi.org/10.1007/978-3-030-00003-5

a running store to get a proper pair of shoes. There, I met more experienced runners and found out about different running events in the area. It was a place I ended up frequenting to ask all sorts of questions about gear and pacing and training. I couldn't believe there was this whole big running world in my own community that I never knew existed.

The eight-mile marathon leg went better than I ever anticipated. In fact, it felt like I was made for this type of physical activity. As soon as I crossed the finish line, I started thinking about what race I could do next. Six months later, I decided to train for Akron's 2nd annual marathon. But this time, I'd do it all myself. My first full marathon that year went well and I wanted to do it again. But, the next time, I wanted to do it better and faster.

Instead of jumping right back into training though, I stepped away from running for a few years; I had a young family and also attended graduate school while working full-time. Through those years at work, I gained responsibilities and began managing a team of people. In order to learn more about operations and make connections with ops people in the industry, I also began attending yearly conferences.

During the conferences, I'd seek out other professionals in similar roles in RIA firms across the country. This is where I realized how much more about operations I had to learn: like what it takes to run the operations of a billion dollar firm (which we weren't at the time); how to achieve scale in a growing advisory firm; and how influential a culture of professionalism focused on serving clients can be for maintaining a productive work environment. In a way, these conferences felt like being at the running store, a place where I could ask all my questions to those with more experience.

Each year, I looked forward to going. Yes, I enjoyed the sessions led by industry superstars. But many of us also craved time to sit around a table with regular people and talk with others like us who were running growing RIA firms and faced similar challenges as we did. It felt like there was this whole world of people who were willing to help and were interested in the same issues. Why weren't we meeting more often or sharing information to help each other on a regular basis?

After each conference, I'd leave a little bit baffled. Because no matter how much we enjoyed it and valued our time together, every year was the same: *Hey, this has been awesome. Wish we could do this more.* And then we'd shake hands and say goodbye. We all knew two days out of an entire year is hardly enough for support and connection and opportunity to learn everything each of us needed, especially at the rate so many of us were growing. It didn't matter, though. We'd return to our jobs and plug away. Sure, we could call or email each other, but there just wasn't an easy way to connect on a broader scale.

While our company grew and a lot more work came through, I, as the operations manager, continued to face new challenges. I had to answer questions such as what were the best ways to consistently train the team on our new technology, how to efficiently onboard our new hires, and how the best firms utilize workflows within their CRM systems. Not only did I apply my knowledge from my MBA, but I took the initiative to learn as much as I could about management and leadership by meeting with nearby executives, reading books, and modeling what I saw my successful colleagues doing.

I liked working with our management team to set a goal and then work to break it down into smaller pieces, identifying what needed to get done, and systematically working on each part until the process, procedure or project was realized. Just like with running, I found the challenge enjoyable and thrived within the discipline of working toward the accomplishment.

Seven years after my first marathon and established in my role at work, I ran a second and then a third marathon. Around this time, I started casually running with a small group of guys, a few of whom were actually podium finishers at Akron's marathon. I met them through friends and I honestly felt like they were humoring me by letting me run with them. I couldn't keep up with their pace, so we'd start to run and after a few miles, I'd tire and they'd go ahead—getting 20, 30, 40 yards out. Inevitably, one would turn around—still running—and yell, "Come on Shaun, catch me! You can do this!" I didn't want to, but they'd keep yelling until I tried. And many times, I did catch them. It wasn't formal coaching. These guys were my buddies. But running with them pushed me beyond what I thought were my own limits.

Out of these challenging training runs, my confidence grew to where I started to wonder if I was able to run a full marathon at a much faster pace. Could it be that I was holding myself back? I felt like I was at a fork in the road: do I keep running the way I'm running, enjoying doing marathons as I have been or do I push myself beyond what I think I'm capable of, just to see if it's possible?

I decided to test the waters by running a half marathon at a 6:30/mile pace. I was more surprised than anyone when I finished strong. Isn't it funny how we don't really realize what we can do until we try? After this, I set a new goal to qualify to run the Boston Marathon.

Two years later, after pushing my speed training at longer and longer distances, in my 5th marathon, I wrote my goal time on the bottom of my shoes on race day and did it.

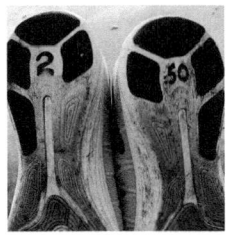Through those years of intense training, our company continued to expand. More and more work was coming to our operations department due to our firm's growth and I did my best with the experience I had to manage the people, the processes, and the technology. But I felt frustrated waiting for the conference each year to connect with others in my position. I had questions about how to integrate technology and I wanted to learn what other people were doing to manage change and keep up with fast growth.

I knew there were a lot of advisors who participated in study groups, so in 2010 I decided to join one of the industry's operations study groups. I spent six months scouring the internet and asking all of my industry contacts to point me toward one focused on RIA operations. But I came up with nothing. It turns out, the industry didn't have a study group for operations professionals at the time. I was looking for something that didn't exist.

Enter: another fork in the road. I could either say "oh well, I guess I'll just keep plugging along as I am" or do the work and figure out how to make an operations study group happen on my own. Knowing what a benefit it would be to me, my firm, my colleagues, clients, and our entire industry, I decided to test the waters.

I reached out to five firms with whom I had connections and said, "I'm interested in having a best practices study group and I'd love for you to join." For me it was simple: we understand each other's issues, challenges, and we're familiar with each other's roles. I was confident that we all had questions—and answers—that would benefit the entire group. At the conference, we would do round tables, so my idea was that we'd invest an hour a month for a virtual round table conference call.

It started with six of us meeting monthly. It didn't take long for one person to tell a connection about our group and asked if that colleague could join. Within a few months, the group began to grow organically and within a year, we doubled in size. We welcomed anyone who wanted to attend to both learn and contribute. It snowballed from there. In 2013, I named the group HIFON (High Impact Financial Operations Network) and by 2017 there were 170 member firms participating.

I knew there was a need for operational networking and for an organized group to connect RIA operations professionals, but what I didn't anticipate was that there would actually be a demand for it. What started as a simple way to grow and build opportunities for professional success morphed into a personal mission: to help each member find their own success. When each person shares their experiences, we all learn. We all grow. We all get better.

I enjoy the process of facilitating opportunities for professional development and connection. Just like with running, I am made for this type of work.

As HIFON's membership grew, I received invitations to speak at industry events—and this is how I met Greg. Our discussions focused largely on technology-driven change in growth firms and helping others through the process. Though he comes from the business ownership side and I from operations, we found a mutual passion for sharing our experiences for the benefit of others. We love the process of talking to those in the industry and learning how to do things better, all of which led to this book.

I wrote every chapter here with the same focus I have as I run HIFON. I don't just want a "win-win" situation, I want it to be a WIN x 5.

- *I want YOU to win.* As members share their experiences in HIFON, everyone has the opportunity to ask questions and learn from each other. More knowledge makes you more valuable. Here, we've shared our experiences and you've learned what it takes to manage a big transition for your firm. You've increased your worth because you have access to a collective pool of information and resources.
- *I want US (everyone else participating) to win.* At HIFON, those of us who hear about your experiences end up growing in our own roles because of the information you share. As managers, we become more valuable to our firms and clients. In the same way, we hope that this book will add to the conversation in our industry about the need for operations-focused content. We want to hear your feedback and grow right along with you.
- *I want OUR COMPANIES to win.* We want every member in each firm to benefit from spending time with other industry professionals, which is why HIFON has expanded the group to benefit compliance professionals and formal planning teams as well. Likewise, we want this book to be available to everyone involved at your firm who has an interest in making your M&A event go well.
- *I want OUR CLIENTS to win.* In the end, it's all about the clients. They're the ones we show up to serve each day. We want our shared experiences and answered questions to directly impact the wellbeing of our collective client base.
- And finally, *I want the RIA INDUSTRY to win.* A rising tide raises all the boats, right? When we improve ourselves, our firms, and what we can deliver to our clients, the RIAs of our industry will continue to shine.

When I started to train for my 9th marathon, the last one to date, I knew I'd have to train differently than I had in the past. There was no way around the fact that I am older and my family is busier than ever. But I had enough experience to know what I needed to focus on in order to make the race a success. Instead of running close to 80 miles per week, as I'd done in the past, I ran only 60. Instead of following the prescribed training plans, I focused less on the short runs during the week and more on making sure I had great long runs on the weekends. I went to bed early, ate clean, and trained regularly with my running partners.

I ended up with nearly the exact same results as I did for the races leading up to Boston. I knew what it took for me to run well and feel good. I had the confidence to trust my experience and know what really mattered. In the same vein, we want you to take what we've learned from our M&A experiences and, in time, make it your own.

When I volunteered for that relay leg a few months after I started working at my current firm, I never anticipated that it would be the first step in my journey of becoming a multi-marathon runner. Nor did I *ever* anticipate that those initial connections with operations people across the country at yearly conferences would lead me to be the founder of a national operations network.

We all take one step at a time with the opportunities before us. We all make decisions when we encounter forks in the road. Business owners, like Greg, have a vision for where they want their business to go—and those of us in operations are the people who help make it happen. We have different roles, yet we all set goals and work together for a common purpose. We all want to do the best we can with the task in front of us.

How M&A Tech Integrations Mirror Marathons

- *The first one's the hardest.*
  There's no way around the fact that you're inexperienced. You have no idea what it's going to be like to run 26.2 miles. (Personally, I didn't realize it would be so long and painful—yet also so satisfying.)

  In the same way, bringing two firm's tech systems together is a big, daunting, and sometimes risky event. No matter how much you learn and anticipate and plan, the outcome feels questionable: *Am I going to make it?* The answer is yes. You're prepared and you'll get through it.
- *You aren't doing this alone.*
  Okay, okay. No one runs for you. But—no one really races alone, either. Those who run best have a solid support team—whether that's formal coaching or a training buddy or simply encouragement from family and

friends. There is a myriad of people who are a part of any race. From the organizers to the waterstop volunteers, they all want you to have a great race-day experience.

Similarly, your M&A technology transition and integration takes a full cadre of teammates, vendors, and custodians. They will all work together toward the success of your firm and your clients making this transition.

- *Support is out there.*

  When I started running, I had no idea there were local groups of runners meeting all through the week. When I finally found my own training group, they pushed me to do more than I ever could have on my own.

  We want you to feel prepared, supported, and hopeful by reading this book. And if you're on the operations side, HIFON is a group continually looking for anyone running operations for an RIA to contribute and learn from. Consider yourself invited. You don't have to go at this alone. HIFON can be your tribe, your people, your operations running group.

- *You can do more and better.*

  Yes, marathons are a lot of work. Probably more than I ever anticipated. But whether we're talking running or getting your firm ready for an M&A technology integration, you spend 4-6 months on this journey, preparing many small details in order for you to meet your goal. You connect with your peers to ask questions and learn how you, too, can do this better. In time, you'll learn what works best for you and how to make the process your own.

You and your firm are capable of big things. You are able to bring two independently successful firms together, satisfying the needs of your clients by becoming stronger and better. It's a huge accomplishment to be proud of. And after getting one or two (or nine) under your belt, it's amazing to look back on what you've already done.

Greg and I have both been a part of multiple M&A experiences and continue to work toward new ones. We want this book to be a guide for you. We want our pooled experiences to equip you to move forward with M&A transactions with confidence, feeling encouraged and empowered to get the job done.

We are grateful for the opportunity to help you through this process. We can't run this race for you, but we can teach you what we know and push you to do it better. We're just a little ahead of you on the path, turning around and confidently saying, "Come on! You can do this!"

We know you can.

References

Davis, R., and Mountain, M. (2015) *Your Surefire Guide to CRM Success: No More Leaving Money on the Table*. Advantage Media Group, Charleston, SC, p. 102.

DeVoe & Company (2018) DeVoe RIA Deal Book, Q1 2018. DevoeandCompany. com. https://static1.squarespace.com/static/5410ec1be4b0b9bdbd0cc342/t/5a-da301e0e2e72f61afcb9ac/1524248607148/DeVoe+Dealbook+1Q18+FINAL. pdf. Accessed 8 July 2018.

Drucker, D., and Bruckenstein, J. (2012) *Technology Tools for Today's High-Margin Practice: How Client-Centered Financial Advisors Can Cut Paperwork*. Overhead, and Wasted Hours. Bloomberg Press, New York, Partial List.

ECHELON Partners (2017) 2017 RIA M&A Deal Report. Echelon-Partners.com. Accessed 8 July 2018.

Heath, C., and Heath, D. (2010) *Switch: How to Change Things When Change Is Hard*. The Crown Publishing Group, New York.

Investment Adviser Association & National Regulatory Services (2017) 2017 Evolution Revolution. https://www.investmentadviser.org/publications/evolution-revolution. Accessed 8 Jul 2018.

Johnson, S. (1998) Who Moved My Cheese? an Amazing Way to Deal with Change in Your Work and in Your Life. G. P. Putnam's Sons, New York.

Kitces, M. (2014) What Are the Key Performance Indicators (KPIs) for Your Financial Planning Firm? Kitces.com. https://www.kitces.com/blog/what-are-the-key-performance-indicators-kpis-for-your-financial-planning-firm/. Accessed 1 August 2018.

Peters, T. J., and Waterman, R. H. (2006) *In Search of Excellence: Lessons from America's Best-Run Companies*. Harper Business, New York.

Podesta, C. (2010) *10 Ways to Stand Out from the Crowd*. Triple Nickel Press, Bloomington, IN.

Veres, B. (2016) *The New Profession*. Independent Publisher, p. 22.

Index

GPSR Compliance

The European Union's (EU) General Product Safety Regulation (GPSR) is a set of rules that requires consumer products to be safe and our obligations to ensure this.

If you have any concerns about our products, you can contact us on ProductSafety@springernature.com

In case Publisher is established outside the EU, the EU authorized representative is:

Springer Nature Customer Service Center GmbH
Europaplatz 3
69115 Heidelberg, Germany

Batch number: 10091722

Printed by Printforce, the Netherlands